What I Never Knew When I Said "I Do"

A concise guide to maintaining a
peaceful and loving relationship.

Bolaji Eyo

Onwards and Upwards Publishers

3 Radfords Turf, Cranbrook, Exeter,
EX5 7DX, United Kingdom.
www.onwardsandupwards.org

This first edition published in the United Kingdom by Onwards and Upwards Publishers (2018).

ISBN: 978-1-78815-682-0
Typeface: Sabon LT

Printed in the United Kingdom.

Endorsements

This is a stunning read and a page-turner. Bolaji [describes] what tradition expects of a relationship vs. the reality of how things are. This will help both women and men break free and change their mentality in terms of what is 'expected', and also be able to make a head-start before getting into a serious relationship.

Dee Cole
CEO, kidsdiaryapp.com

I have known Bolaji for almost two decades. From girls, we grew to women. I could relate to many of the stories as I was there, and to others because I'm also in a marriage. We were in relatively similar situations: we got pregnant, then got married.

This book is obviously from her heart, and Bolaji was guided by the Lord. Years of marriage and years of having a truly understanding partner who is willing to work with her all the way have given her the grace to write this.

Anyone who is about to say, "I do!" should read this – and anyone who [is already married will find] help with their relationship.

A truly worthy read.

Dr Fikayo Manuwa
Medical doctor
Blog: thismarriagething.blogspot.uk

About the Author

Bolaji Eyo lives in Hertfordshire with her husband and two lovely daughters. She owns and runs Sophianna's Bakery, a bespoke cake boutique business. Her debut novel, 'Good girls don't put out', was released in January 2017. When she doesn't have her face stuck in a book or writing, she can be found in the kitchen, baking and decorating beautiful cakes. She is also a Certified Business Analyst Professional and has worked as a Business Analyst Consultant for the last ten years.

To contact Bolaji, please send an email to:

Hello@bolajieyo.com

More information can be found at:

www.bolajieyo.com

Acknowledgements

As in everything, God comes first. I believe he put every word of this book upon my heart. And so I thank God for this book; every word was written for me, and as I wrote, I learnt a little more from my past experiences.

I would like to thank Luke and the team at Onwards and Upwards, for giving this book a chance and for doing an incredible job of shaping it. I'm grateful for the time and attention I received during the editing process and for always pointing me in the right direction in moments of indecisiveness.

I wrote this book based on my marriage, and when I started, I was sceptical about how my husband would take it. Knowing him as a private person, I was about to expose intimate details of our relationship. Thank you, Emmanuel Eyo, my husband and my best friend, for your love and unwavering support.

To my mom and dad, thank you for being great marital role models. You showed me what a healthy marriage looked like and gave me an image that I aspire to emulate.

Banke, my one and only sister, thank you for being the best sister anyone could wish to have; for being a great listener and for being there whenever I need you.

My wonderful mother-in-law, I'm grateful for your heart of gold; for your love and support and for always being ready to look after the kids, making regular date nights possible.

My boss, 'S.P.', thank you for your constructive and encouraging feedback.

To Vishal Morjaria and all the members of my writing group, thank you for the regular motivation to finish and publish my book.

Arinola, thank you for agreeing to write my foreword. At a time when you were juggling so much in the air, you made time to add me into the mix.

Esther Godwin, my beta reader, thank you for helping me view this book objectively. You made me believe that this book was worth writing.

To my friends – in particular, Stephanie, Dee, Misi, Sogie, Omo-wunmi and Dr Fikayo – thank you for allowing me to use you as sounding boards, for your great feedback and all your encouragement.

Contents

Foreword by Arinola Nnatuanya

One can read a book and assume they already know what will be said or covered in it. This book, for me, hasn't just been a reminder of things I knew but has also highlighted areas where I can be better in my marriage.

Having been married for fourteen years, one would like to see oneself as having some experience in marriage, and while experience can be a good thing, it can also limit you from growing. This book has given me opportunity to reflect on our relationship and has challenged some of my views and opinions on certain aspects of marriage.

It's a must-read for both the married and unmarried, and has tips on day-to-day life situations that we face in our relationships.

Arinola Nnatuanya
Singer / Songwriter
CEO, Fusion Records

Introduction

WHEN I DECIDED TO WRITE this book, I had no idea what lay ahead. I was sitting at a conference full of coaches and entrepreneurs, listening to a speaker, but as he spoke, the entire outline of the book popped into my head and I wrote the ideas down; they were completely unrelated to what the speaker was saying, but it kept flowing nonetheless. That was the easy part. Fast-forward a couple of months, I had done nothing with the book and so I decided to attend a three-day conference for authors to "get their book done". As I stood up in the room to announce my book title, I said, "I just want to say, I'm not an authority on marriage in any way; I've only been married six years." A stunning blonde lady in front of me turned around and said, "Well, I got divorced after six years!" Another lovely lady to my left piped in, "And I've never been married; I would love to hear what you have to say." So here it is.

The aim of this book isn't to teach you how to find the man with whom you pledge to spend the rest of your life. However, I do hope that by reading this book, you change the way you view marriage and in turn attract your heart's desires. If you've already found him, then I congratulate you! Reading this book may help you avoid some of the pitfalls within a new marriage. Some of these may seem insignificant but even the minor issues have the power to make or break a new marriage.

I have gone through so many changes from the young, carefree and independent lady I was before I met my husband to become the woman that I am now. In my quest to hold on to my identity and independence in my marriage, I have made several mistakes. I'm still learning from them. These are the things I never knew when I said, "I do."

CHAPTER ONE

And Then There Were Two

The ideal spouse

DO YOU HAVE A LIST OF the qualities you want in your partner? I know I did; I never wrote it down but it was etched in my mind. I think prevalent for me was the list I had of the qualities I *didn't* want in my future partner. It wasn't something I'd set out to create; I'd built my list over time based on the previous relationships I had been in or interactions I'd had with the opposite sex. It was also compiled based on what I knew about myself; what I could and couldn't handle in a relationship. It is important before entering a relationship to understand your relationship threshold, that is, what can this person do to me that will make me want (or have) to call it quits?

For example, could I forgive him/her if he/she hits me?

If he/she cheats on me, could we move on?

What if my partner brings another child into my home? Gambles or swindles all our money away?

It's easier to spot the signs when you know what your breaking point is. It doesn't mean that you wouldn't change your mind about what action to take.

I guess I was lucky enough to have been involved in a few unlucky relationships before I met my husband.

I was nineteen when I had my first boyfriend. I did all the calling. I travelled to see him all the time and after a while it started to feel one-sided and more work than it was worth. Every time I went to see him, a particular girl was always there; he said she was his friend. It didn't matter that I'd travelled to his school to see him, she never excused herself and he never asked her to leave – so I left him. They started

11

dating months after. The relationship made me feel desperate; it was a terrible feeling, and so I promised myself that I would never stay in a relationship that made me desperate.

My next relationship, we started out as friends and then it became complicated. He said he liked me but I wasn't ready for a relationship. Until one day I realised that I liked him and I wanted more and so I told him. All of a sudden, he could do without me and I couldn't live without him.

I tried to keep my promise to myself. I didn't want to seem desperate but I didn't want to leave either, and so I pretended that everything was fine. It was okay that I couldn't come over because he had another female friend around and it would be uncomfortable and awkward for him, even though they were just friends. It was okay that he could call me when he was broke or needed a lift somewhere, that I would drop everything to be there for him. It was all right that I missed lectures to look after him when he was ill, tending to his every whim, and yet when he was better I could never seem to reach him on the phone.

I pretended to be alright when my friends told me about 'this or that girl' he was seeing. It was all fine as long as no one saw me as desperate... desperately clinging on to nothing. I knew he was bad for me, I saw all the signs, but I thought we would be together forever because that was what he said. He told me he could see us together, going to functions together in matching outfits, growing old together. At the time, the thought of marriage hadn't even crossed my mind. Before then, my view of marriage was that it was a long, boring and loveless relationship and it wasn't something I particularly aspired to, however, the picture he painted enticed me; I ate it all up. I held on to it and wouldn't let go even when it seemed to be in vain. He would surely come to his senses and realise that I was good for him – scratch that, I was *perfect* for him – that I could make him happy, I would always be there, no matter what.

He made me laugh and I felt so alive when I was with him, but when I wasn't with him, I was miserable. I couldn't call him just to talk. He would accuse me of calling him only because I was bored. I had to have an *important* reason for calling.

Then he started dating someone else. No warning. It hurt, and it was hard to let go even then. My friend thought I was crazy or stupid – or both. The thing is, when you see a beautiful picture with someone and you've invested so much in the relationship, it's not so easy to let go. In the end, I found the strength and the distance to move on. The lessons I learnt from that relationship were to never let any man walk all over me, to only date financially independent men and to never lose my integrity.

Note that in the points above, I mentioned that I promised myself that I would only date financially independent men. I wasn't looking for a rich guy or a sugar daddy; all I wanted was for the man to be able to hold his own. When you're in love, it's easy to waive the financial aspect, choosing to help a man until he is on his feet. And not that there's anything wrong with that, but if he seems comfortable with you trying to help him financially, then there's your red flag. If you find yourself 'helping him out' with unnecessary and vain expenses (basically, he's not desperately in need) and he lets you, you will find yourself carrying him on your back for a long time. The signs are mostly always there at the start of the relationship. The question is, are you going to do anything about it?

I've given these examples to highlight how important it is to understand what you're willing to accept in a relationship before you get in too deep. As soon as you see the signs, hightail it out of there as fast as you can. If your man puts his hand on you once, it is almost certain that he will do it again. Not only is abuse physical, it can also be financial and psychological. Trust your instincts and never look back. Never let the fear of being alone thrust you into an abusive marriage.

"What is your ideal man?" someone once asked me.

"Ooh, he has to be tall, dark and handsome," I responded, stealing the clichéd description from nearly every Mills and Boon novel I ever read.

"No," my friend said, rolling her eyes. "I mean, what characteristics do you want in a man?"

"Well," I thought, bringing to mind descriptions I had picked up from all the romantic movies I had seen, "I guess I would like him to be sensitive and kind."

I know... I was hopeless.

In reality, I didn't think it was necessary to have a list; when I met the right person, I would just know. I learnt the hard way. By the time I met my husband, not only did I know what I wanted, but I also knew what I didn't want, and it was based on my past experiences with the opposite sex. As I grew older and more experienced, it was easier to spot the signs and as soon as I did, I ran, regardless of how strong the attraction was. In 'Reawaken the Giant Within', a book by life coach Tony Robbins, he talks about how people are motivated either towards what will give pleasure or away from what would cause pain. And so the thought of a repeat of some of those experiences gave me the strength I needed to call it quits no matter how happy I thought I was with that person. In most instances, I didn't bother discussing it or trying to change him; I just ran. He never heard from me, I never picked up his calls. This approach isn't the best when it comes to leaving a relationship, but I was young then. As young and naïve as I was, I was smart enough to know myself. Those men were smooth talkers and I wasn't about to give them a chance to break down my defences while I was still vulnerable. I was called hard, cold and heartless; deep inside I knew I was the exact opposite but it was the only way I knew to protect my heart.

List the experiences from your past relationship that you would like to avoid in your current or future relationship. It could even be something that happened to someone you know or on TV.

1. _____

2. _____

3. _____

4. _____

Writing this down will help you spot the signs early on before you get in too deep. You can refer to it over time to remind you not to settle.

I recall a conversation I had with a dear friend of mine, Funke, almost eight years ago. She had just had a big fight with her then boyfriend.

It was night time, I had gone to visit her and she was walking me to catch my bus back home. The mood was solemn as she listed all the reasons she had to leave her boyfriend. And I agreed with her.

"I would never say this to anyone, and I hope you don't hate me for it, but you have to break up with him," I said.

"I can't; I'm already in my mid-twenties. What if I never meet anyone else? He loves me; I know he does," she said, doing a complete 180 degrees as soon as she saw I wasn't going to convince her to stick it out.

"I don't think it's enough; this, what you have, it's not healthy. You're unhappy with him; doesn't that count for something?"

"Yes, but I'm unhappy *without* him."

"I understand, but that unhappy feeling will pass with time. You're beautiful, kind, amazing. I promise you'll be fine."

"I can't," she insisted and then she sighed. "I'm just not like you. We'll be fine."

Funke and her boyfriend got married that year, and three years later the marriage was over.

"I'm so sorry I didn't listen to you," she said to me afterwards. "I could have saved myself the heartache."

Settling with the wrong guy just to get married is just not worth it. Ask anyone in an unhappy or abusive marriage. Before you get married, you need to be honest with yourself about your 'why'.

Why are you getting married? Are you pregnant? If, God forbid, you lost the pregnancy, would that sound the death knell to your marriage?

Why him? Is he rich? If he lost all his money tomorrow, where would that leave your marriage?

List all your reasons for getting married, and then subtract them from the equation. If you had nothing left, would you remain together? How hard will you fight for your marriage when it feels like you've got nothing to fight for? It's not an easy question to answer, but you should be willing to give it a try before jumping in. Make your mind up about wanting your marriage to survive. Too many marriages break up because of pride or the illusion that marriage is a bed of roses. It can be, but you have to be willing to deal with the thorns. Some people will live with it, accepting the uncomfortable pricks and jabs and do nothing about it. Some people will go out and buy pruning shears, trimming at those thorns; they might not get rid of all the thorns, and sometimes the thorns grow back, but they keep pruning, refusing to give up. And then there are those people that will just walk away; they didn't anticipate the thorns, it wasn't what they signed up for, so no one can blame them when they just decide they can't handle it anymore. You have to decide which category you fall into: the thorn-bearer, the thorn-pruner, or the thorn-averse.

What is on your Ideal Spouse list?

1. _____

2. _____

3. _____

4. _____

5. _____

Why is/was your reason for getting married?

According to Genesis, man was made to have dominion over all the earth and the woman was made to be his companion.

> *Then the LORD God made a woman from the rib he had taken out of the man, and he brought her to the man. The man said, "This is now bone of my bones and flesh of my flesh; she shall be called 'woman,' for she was taken out of man." That is why a man leaves his father and mother and is united to his wife, and they become one flesh.*
>
> *Genesis 2:22-24*

As human beings, we are prone to human desires and so...

> *...because of the temptation to sexual immorality, each man should have his own wife and each woman her own husband.*
>
> *1 Corinthians 7:2 (ESV)*

What is your 'why'?

My husband and I got married two and a half weeks after our first child was born. The general feeling was that we got married because we had a child. The thing is, we'd initially planned the wedding for when I was five months pregnant before the signs started showing, to hide the shame or for whatever reason. We bought the dress, it fitted perfectly, not too snug, so that I could grow into it, and it had folds and other decorative distractions around the waist, just in case there was a telltale bulge. We went round to look at wedding venues and just as we were about to place a deposit on a beautiful hall we had found within our price range, we realised we were making a mistake. From the moment we had decided to get married, we knew this was something we were doing for other people and not for us. This decision that was supposed to make our friends, families and church members happy was making us miserable. We loved each other, but no one wants to be forced to do anything before they feel ready.

What are your reasons for getting married? To be happy? So that people will stop asking you, "So when are you getting married?" like you have the power to make the man appear out of thin air? You feel time is running out; you're getting desperate, loved ones are cruel and insensitive towards you. Then you meet a guy and all you can think of is that trip to the altar, so you ignore the warning signs. If you are not already married, ask your "why" now and be truthful to yourself. Whatever your response is, be sure that you can live with it.

My husband and I had to face the truth; the only reason we were getting married was because I was pregnant. If there wasn't a baby on the way, marriage would have been further from our minds. At the rate we were going, we were going to tear each other apart because we were both afraid. Neither of us wanted to get married, and instead of being brave and saying something, the friction and the tension grew until it had to be tackled. A once blissful relationship became rife with bitterness and suspicion until we were able to step back and pinpoint the root cause of the storm that threatened our relationship.

Calling off the wedding was hard and scary, but I was taken aback by the love and support we received from the same people we expected to judge us. A part of me was afraid: what if we never got married? I would become a single mom; it would be that much harder for me to get out there and find another man. The other part of me was relieved; I felt that if we had continued down our previous path, a broken marriage would have been inevitable.

It took some work for us to get to the place where we felt ready to get married, not because of the child we were having or because of any external pressure but because we believed that God had chosen us to be together and that he would forever be the third strand in our relationship, binding us together, stronger than any force on earth.

So when people ask me if I got married because I was pregnant, I say, "Yes, I probably wouldn't be married to my husband if I hadn't become pregnant, but that is not the *reason* we got married." Getting pregnant meant there was more at stake and it helped us to fight harder for our relationship in situations where it would have been easier to walk away.

Expecting a baby taught us to be patient with one another. It broke down my stubborn and independent streak (to a certain extent) and changed me. I needed that transformation to be ready for marriage; we both did. God needed to humble and transform us, to break us down and mould us so that we were completely compatible, fitting into each other in just the right places.

What are/were your reasons for getting married?

1. _____

2. _____

3. _____

4. _____

5. _____

Planning for marriage

Before you embark on a business, a journey or even going into labour, you're encouraged to have a plan. I'm not one for planning; how to do you plan for childbirth or a journey when there are so many things that can go wrong?

With my first child, I refused to have a plan, and I practically packed a bag the day I went into the hospital. It just didn't make sense to me to plan so far in advance. I mean, come on, you go in the labour ward, the baby either comes out naturally or the doctors decide it has to be taken out either by caesarean with forceps or a suction cup. You can decide on painkillers based on how you feel at the time. It was so much better to 'wing it' so that no matter how things went, I wouldn't be disappointed. That was my plan anyway. *It was a terrible plan.*

I grew up in Lagos, Nigeria and planning for the future was a foreign concept to me. Have you ever heard of African time? Guess what? It stems from inadequate planning. When you live in an environment where everything seems to be out of your control, the only thing you can do is pray that things go your way. Planning just further reinforces your feeling of failure when it all goes to pot. Planning to attend a wedding on time? Well, so many factors are in your way, from the lack of electricity to iron your clothes, to torrential rains destroying your outfit (yeah, no one checks the weather before heading out, it's so unpredictable anyway); not to mention fuel scarcity and terrible traffic – stuck in your car in 38°C weather. For me, birthday parties were strung together either the day before or on the same day. Outings were spontaneous; I've even booked holidays with less than a day's notice. Booking a holiday in advance still feels odd, like a recipe for disaster.

I certainly didn't plan for my marriage.

I *do* mean marriage, of course, not the wedding. I *did* plan the wedding! But I wish I had planned for my marriage. By plan, I don't mean a schedule; I mean, to think about the kind of marriage I wanted.

I knew the kind of man I wanted to marry; it was high on my priority list. He had to have certain qualities. But if you'd asked what kind of relationship I wanted, I would have struggled to reply.

If you can, write down what you want from your marriage. What kind of relationship do you want? Is it from something you saw in a movie or read in a book, or the kind of marriage you've seen modelled in real life?

_____

_____

_____

You might be wondering why I'm asking you to do this. Well, we humans are fickle creatures and we change our minds depending on our circumstances.

In the early years of our marriage, I was happy enough but I knew something was missing. We were struggling with a new baby, a new home, we were both contractors and so we were in and out of work; we barely had time for one another. We knew something was missing but we never thought to address it. Left to me, it would have never occurred to analyse and evaluate our marriage. I thank God every day for the wisdom he imparted in my husband and the drive in him to be passionate about the success of our relationship.

"We need to go out, just you and me. We haven't been out in a long time," he said to me one day.

I could think of ten reasons on the spot why we couldn't go out. Even if we could afford going out, we couldn't afford childcare. But I saw his point; it was almost impossible to have a conversation in the house, there was always one distraction or another, and the new wife and mother that I was, I was a busybody, trying to carry the household all by myself. The only time I wasn't doing anything was when I was asleep!

We were lucky to have good family friends living close by so we bundled our daughter off, and armed with Groupon vouchers, we set out to an Italian restaurant.

"What do you want from this marriage?" my husband asked as we tucked into our meal.

His question stumped me. What did it matter what I wanted? This was what I had and I had to work with it.

"No, I mean, is this the *kind* of marriage you want? Are you happy?" He proceeded to list the type of marriage he wanted and the plans he had, and as he spoke, I realised that I had never allowed myself to even think about it and I started to come up with what I wanted as well.

That evening, we mapped out our plans for our marriage. It would take some work on both our parts but it was exciting. We were working towards a better future for ourselves. Instead of just sitting back and letting life happen to us, instead of just existing in a marriage, we were working on a plan to have the life of our dreams. And it had nothing to do with what we had or wanted to have. It had nothing to do with our dream house or our dream car. It was realising that it was two of us 'in this together'; there was no going back and it was up to us that we made it less like a prison sentence and more like paradise.

Another more recent occurrence made me re-evaluate my view on marriage. One morning, I was listening to a colleague explain why she had been late for work. The kids were on holiday and since she didn't have to do the school run, she and her husband had spent extra time in bed, just 'cuddling'. Apparently, they liked to 'cuddle' in the mornings.

My jaw dropped as I listened to her. Here was a woman who had been married for over twelve years and she like to cuddle with her husband in the mornings.

"I wish my husband and I did that," I mumbled in awe as I thought how stressed our mornings were. As soon as the words left my lips, a question popped into my head: why don't we do it, what is stopping us? The answer was, *nothing*. It was at that moment that I realised that my marriage could be anything I wanted it to be. I started dreaming up my ideal marriage, things I could do to work towards building a marriage that I wanted, ways I could change.

- I wanted to be happy with my husband in the morning.

This meant no loaded looks because he 'didn't get up in time' and thus, due to the logistics of two grown-ups and two little kids sharing a bathroom, we would have less time to get the kids ready for school.

- I wanted to pay more attention to him when he got home in the evening.

I cast my mind back to the early years of our marriage when he would come in from work and I would barely glance his way as I worked, flustered, in the kitchen, trying to balance being a mom and a wife after being at work for eight hours. Resentment bubbled in my chest over his relaxed demeanour as he took his time getting changed from his work clothes and getting settled in while I bustled around the kitchen still in my work clothes. I ignored his gentle protests that I didn't give him any attention. I realised that I had stopped hearing those protests years ago and it was with alarm that I recognised that we had both found other things to fill up our time with apart from one another.

- I wanted to be able to talk about anything that bothered me.

This meant no more walking around the house with a cloud of doom hanging over my head, waiting for him to ask me, "What's wrong?" so that I could pounce.

Have a conversation with your spouse about how you would like to change to improve your marriage, for the sake of accountability. Be careful not to demand that he do the same; in fact, stress that it is a change *you* would like to make and leave it to him to decide what he would like to do to improve your relationship. Take it one step further and ask if there's anything *he* would like you to do differently. Once again, wait till he asks you before you volunteer what you would like him to do. The last thing you want to do is make him feel manipulated, as if you're doing this only to further your own agenda.

What can you change about your current habits with your spouse to make your home environment not only conducive but a place you can't wait to get back to at the end of the day?

It could be little things like: I want us to kiss whenever we say goodbye or hello; I like cuddles in the morning before getting out of bed; I want my husband to hold me affectionately when we're out in public. It could even be the opposite: "I'm uncomfortable with public displays of affection, and so I would like to be touched only in private."

Model your plan according to what <u>you</u> want. Don't think of someone else's marriage. The people in that marriage are not you. Fill in your marriage plan, working through the exercise with your spouse.

If you are not married yet:
Write down your vision for your marriage

1. _____

2. _____

3. _____

4. _____

If you are married:
Write down what you would like to do differently to improve your relationship with your spouse.

1. _____

2. _____

3. _____

4. _____

Living your ideal marriage

You and your spouse are responsible for the success of your marriage. It is not just your responsibility, nor is it solely your spouse's, to ensure the success of your relationship. Therefore, it is important that we enter with the intention of giving ourselves to our partners, in a similar way that Christ gave himself to the church.

When I was getting married, I thought it was all about me: my happiness, my stuff, my space, my money... I'd heard so many wrong views about marriage that I had my guard up. I had to protect myself from getting cheated on, financially, emotionally, psychologically. I had expectations from my spouse as well, things I deserved, things he was meant to provide for me... Every piece of foolish advice I'd ever heard drifted through my mind.

And now I have come to realise that none of those things are important; none of them matter. I'm in this relationship for the rest of my life no matter what happens, in wealth and lack, in sickness and good form. This is it... for life!

When I was single, I never thought about how I wanted my married life to look. If pushed, I would have created a model formed from my parents' marriage. True, I'd thought about the wedding; I wanted a small wedding, with only our closest friends and family. I'd thought about the type of house I wanted to live in, how many kids we would have... but I had never really focused on the kind of relationship I wanted to have with my partner.

It might seem unimportant now but it's easier at the beginning of a relationship or a marriage to form patterns that will shape your future. Discussing the type of relationship you want early on will give you a better chance of getting it. It's easy to fall into a rut and to take the other person for granted in a long-term relationship like a marriage.

Believe that you can have the marriage you want and work towards it with purpose and intention in the way you relate with one another.

Chapter Two

What Is Love?

DURING MY TEENS, MY HEAD was constantly stuck in a novel, so much so that in secondary school it became part of my description: *The girl that's always with novel.* That four-letter word, *love,* came up often in those books. And in them, that moment when someone says, "I love you," was always so special. I could feel what the characters in my book felt; there was passion and there was desire. Blood rushing, emotions stirring, adrenaline pulsing and endorphins intoxicating.

I searched for that feeling in my relationships, so when I got those heady feelings, I believed it was love. I said, "I love you," with adrenaline gushing through me, infusing my chest with an exciting warmth that made me truly believe that this was what love felt like. It never lasted, no matter how much I wanted it to. The fact that I said, "I love you," meant you had to stay, that I had to do everything in my power to *make* you stay. The thing I realised is that in a relationship it takes two people. When one person is absent from the mix, it's called 'unrequited love'.

When I met the man I was going to marry, I believe that the decision to love not only came from our hearts or our attraction to one another, it also came from our heads. It was everything I'd dreamed of and more, and I remember feeling like I'd won the lottery at the time. So *we* made a decision to commit to one another, to start a relationship.

Love was a decision to make. You can choose to love one person and to fall out of love with another. I'm not referring to an obsession or an infatuation; I'm talking about love. The problem is, too many people, like I did, are getting their definition of love from movies and novels, when the true definition can be found in the greatest book ever written: the Bible.

> *Love is patient, love is kind. It does not envy, it does not boast, it is not proud. It does not dishonour others, it is not self-seeking, it is not easily angered, it keeps no record of wrongs. Love does not delight in evil but rejoices with the truth. It always protects, always trusts, always hopes, and always perseveres. Love never fails.*
>
> *1 Corinthians 13:4-8*

People who are *in love* make promises, like, "I'll do anything for you. I'll catch a grenade for you."

Some people base their definition of love on material things. "He didn't buy me this, so that means he doesn't love me." But this is just *their* definition of love.

For some people it's the passion, and when it's gone, they claim to have fallen out of love.

Passion is fickle, money burns, none of it is permanent. How do people still expect love based on such things to last? Personally, I don't *feel* like I love my husband every day. Sometimes I have to make a *decision* to love him; to love him according to the one true definition of love.

Make a conscious decision to love your spouse. And hopefully your spouse's definition of love aligns with yours; the last thing you want is a spouse to whom love means turning you into a punching bag.

What are you bringing to the table?

You're sitting across the table from your potential boss in a job interview, and then the question comes up. The chances are that you have your answer memorised. You're prepared for the interview and you already anticipated the question. The interviewer wants to know what other extras they will be getting when they get you.

In relation to your marriage, this doesn't include the things that *should* come with a relationship such as affection, trust, attention, etc. What will you contribute to the relationship to ensure that the relationship succeeds?

Someone I used to date once said to me, "I want to be the best boyfriend you've ever had, or will ever have, so that whoever comes after me will have his work cut out for him." At the time, I was amazed that anyone could make such a bold statement, but he was right. I met my husband soon after and, according to him, it was the hardest he'd ever had to work at a relationship. I'd become used to a standard that I wasn't willing to let go of: "You either live up to the standard or leave so that I can find someone who can." I wasn't settling when it came to how I was treated in the relationship. Now I can say that my husband is the best husband I will ever have. But it doesn't end with expecting it. I want him to feel the same way as well. I want the thought of him living without me to fill him with dread. I want to be the best wife to him so much that if he were ever tempted to leave (heaven forbid), whoever comes after me would have her work cut out for her.

Are you able to say that to your spouse? That you know without a doubt that if he/she were to leave you today, they would struggle to find someone who would love them as much or treat them as well as you do?

If you can't, maybe it's time to start working on how you perceive your spouse. It may be that you take your spouse for granted. Are there any blockers, mainly emotional blockers, preventing you from achieving this? Are you holding onto resentment? Chapter 6 is about letting go of any resentment against your spouse.

What is it that you know they would love? Your attention? Maybe block out some time in the day where phones are not allowed except in emergencies.

In the movie 'War Room', a husband asks his wife what she wants and she responds jokingly that she would like a foot massage and ice cream at the same time. Throughout the movie, we've been shown just how badly her feet stink; at one point she gives up trying to spray her designer shoes with deodorant and throws them all out. At the end of the movie, he surprises her with the flavour of ice cream she wanted and gives her a foot massage but with a mask over his nose to bear the odour of her feet. It wasn't just about the act – she could have easily paid for ice cream and a foot massage – but him doing it showed how much he loved and appreciated her.

What can you do for your spouse today and every day to show them that you're the best partner for them in the whole world?

Write down seven things. Don't stop there. Write one down for each day. Keep adding to it and mixing it up. Watch what happens to your relationship.

1. _____

2. _____

3. _____

4. _____

5. _____

6. _____

7. _____

Where does your marriage lie on your priority list?

Everyone that enters into a partnership is making a commitment. You're either committed to making your marriage a success or a failure. Your level of commitment also has everything to do with the value you place on that partnership.

How you treat your marriage depends on where your marriage ranks on your priority list, doesn't it? And of course, if you took a survey, ninety-nine out of a hundred people would probably put it way up there, just under God. I know I would.

Recently, I began to realise that I was a hypocrite. I would state with great passion how my marriage was very important to me but, in all honesty, I was giving it less attention than I gave the kids or work or – dare I admit? – the TV. If my husband started a conversation during my favourite show, my first reaction would be one of annoyance, and then guilt, before I would pick up the remote and hit the pause button. Or, when working, I'd stop what I was doing, reluctantly, to give him my undivided attention – at least, as far as he knew; my mind was barely on his words and more on the heap of work I had to get done before bedtime and the fact that my feet were already aching.

How high is your marriage on your priority or value list? If the values of the things on your priority list were graded according to how much time you spent on them, where would your marriage fit on your list?

Like Martha, I'm much too busy to indulge in spending time with my husband; there's important work to get done! In Luke 10:41-42, Jesus said to her:

> *Martha, Martha, you are worried and upset about many things, but few things are needed – or indeed only one. Mary has chosen what is better, and it will not be taken away from her.*

I'm learning to be less reluctant, to let the work wait for a few minutes to give my husband attention when he needs it. When the job is done, I need him to want to leave whatever he's doing to spend time with me also. I want to feel that I am important to him and I should be willing to do the same for him.

When you meet 'the one'

When I met my husband, we both knew we were going to be together. I remember telling a mutual friend that I felt it was too good to be true. I'd had too many disappointing experiences from previous relationships and so I'd put up strong emotional barriers to protect myself from the inevitable. I did not expect that it would last, only because it was more intense than I was used to. This was a good thing, but to me at the time, it just felt like too much work. I was used to being free to do whatever I pleased, go wherever I wanted. I had never been in a relationship where the other person communicated so clearly or openly about how they felt about my actions. I was used to playing games, the "you hurt me, and so I'll hurt you back so you can have a taste of your own medicine" kind of relationship.

It was frightening. Here I was in a relationship with a man that ticked all my boxes, yet I wanted a way out! I tried to disentangle myself but one way or another we kept finding our way back. I remember asking him why he didn't just give up and call it quits, and he had no idea; it was frustrating for him as well but something kept pushing us back together.

Looking back, I believe it was a result of all the years of praying for my future husband. When God chooses your man, he will keep coming back to you.

I had to change who I was to make it work. The person I was before was not ready to settle down; no matter how much I said it, my heart didn't believe it. I was independent and stubborn. In my previous relationships, my character had been accepted as who I was, and those relationships had been less than ideal. No one was communicating what the other party was doing wrong or right. It was almost like a competition to see who could hurt the other person more and come out smelling of roses.

For example, imagine the following scenario.

My husband says to me, "Is it alright if I go out for dinner with Rhoda [an ex-girlfriend]? She's only in town for a few days and it would be nice to see her before she leaves."

I reply, "Oh, that's okay. Would she like to come over for dinner so I can meet her?"

"No, no, it'll be too awkward. We'll just go out."

"Fine," I respond. "Say hi for me. You know..." Instead of telling how I really feel, I fold my arms and stroke my chin. Then I add, "You know, Joe [an ex-boyfriend] is in town next week. If you're going to meet Rhoda, that means I can hang out with him. You don't have a problem with that, do you?"

At this point, my poker face is on. If he says, "Sure, go! No problem!" then I'm in trouble; I haven't been honest in telling him how I feel.

Speak with your husband openly. Communication is key here; tell him how you feel about him meeting up with his ex-girlfriend. How would he feel if you did the same? And if it's not an issue for him, let him know that it *is* for you, and that you would rather he didn't. If he loves and respects you, the last thing he should want is to hurt you.

Sex before marriage

You already know that I had a child before marriage, so who am I to talk, right? Don't switch off on me yet, though; just hear me out. God has given us free will; it's up to you to make your own decisions, and it's up to me to share my mistakes even if it is to save just one person from making the same choice.

The media has flooded our minds with so many false messages. The message to men is that a woman who doesn't want to have sex with you is wasting your time or is just playing games. The message for women is that no man will stick around if you're not having sex with him. So we've come roundabout to the point where, as I mentioned earlier, we're modelling our lives around what we watch on our TV screens. Never mind your mother, she's ancient, living in a generation that isn't 'current' or 'happening'. She couldn't possibly understand how hard it is to keep a man in this generation.

Let me ask you this: how many of the men you slept with stayed? I mean, before the one you're with now. If sex was the glue that held your relationship together, how come they left anyway? (Or maybe you left.) If he won't stick around because of lack of sex, the chances are that he won't stick around no matter how skilled you think you are in the bedroom. We think that there's always that one that might just stick around – but why put ourselves through all that?

If you have a relationship with God, then you know what the Bible says about fornication. So, after sex with a man who is not your husband, you feel dirty, afraid to come before God, clothed in your sin. (If you have no qualms about going into God's presence while committing fornication, or any sin for that matter, showing no remorse, then it says something about your relationship with God.)

I'm sharing my story because I hope that it encourages you if you're struggling to remain firm.

When I met my husband, he believed in God, however, at that point in his life, he didn't have a personal relationship with God. He started to come to church with me. We both knew that what we were doing was wrong and one day we had a discussion about it. As a result of our conversation, we made a decision to stop and wait until after we got married. If felt ironic the next day to discover that perhaps we'd made our decision about a month too late.

Even though I was pregnant, we stuck to our decision to remain steadfast until after we were married. It was the first time I'd dared having that discussion with anyone I'd dated and it was only because I felt secure in the relationship and I knew that what we had went way beyond the physical attraction. In my previous relationships, I was too insecure, afraid that my boyfriend would leave me if sex wasn't on the table. *And they probably would have* – but if this is how you feel, you should try having this conversation. If your man really loves you, I promise you, nothing will keep him away.

Apparently, we were both on the same wavelength, but no one wanted to offend the other by bringing it up. Letting go of sexual intimacy helped us focus more on our relationship. I believe that waiting increases the level of intimacy in marriage; I also believe that it further instils in you that sex should never be the main focus in a relationship.

CHAPTER THREE

Your Spouse Is Not Your Ex

THE REASON YOUR SPOUSE BEHAVES a certain way may be different to the reasons someone else you know acted that way.

Let's say your ex-boyfriend was terrible; he cheated on you, never called when he said he would, and did a host of other not very nice things to you. Or your sister's husband brought another woman into his matrimonial home and squandered all your sister's money, leaving them facing repossession of their home. Whatever sins the men of the world commit, do not to take it out on your spouse. Your husband should not be paying for the sins of others.

The stories you hear about other relationships can creep into your head and affect the way you treat your husband or the way you react to something he does, which in different circumstances would not have been a big deal.

Every relationship deserves a clean slate; not one piled with the sins of the men in your past or in your life. Otherwise, you'll only end up hurting yourself and the one you love. It's important to communicate what hurt you've had in the past so that your spouse is sensitive to it.

My friend, Vivian, had a bad experience in a previous relationship; her ex-boyfriend cheated on her with a couple of her friends. Even though she's moved on and is in a healthy marriage, every time she spots her husband talking to her friends, she's always on high alert. Her husband, Francis, is aware of his wife's feelings and so he makes an effort to keep a minimum distance between himself and any of her friends in any situation, even when she's not there. *Especially* when she's not there. He doesn't keep her friends' phone numbers and doesn't make casual calls to them. This is a sign of respect to his wife and to her feelings. Sometimes it's the other way round; the husband is traumatised by the events in his past relationships. It is up to you to continue to love and respect your spouse, being sensitive to their insecurities until such a time that the trust they have in you is solid.

What are the things you hold against your husband even though you know it's not his fault?

1. _____

2. _____

3. _____

4. _____

5. _____

In the early years of our marriage, my husband and I used to get frustrated by our insecurities. Unless you discuss your insecurities with your spouse, it'll be difficult for him to understand. I used to get upset; I didn't understand why my husband didn't trust me. For example, I noticed he gave me a funny look whenever I placed my phone face down on the table. Apparently, it had worried him for a while as he had a friend who did that because he was cheating on his girlfriend. Unfortunately, by the time he asked me, it had eaten into his mind. And so even though he asked cautiously, I could sense the paranoia in his voice. I was upset by the fact that he thought I was trying to hide something from him, even though I leave my phone lying around and I don't have a lock on it. I try not to have conversations when I'm upset so I didn't respond; I just ignored him. "Good for him," I thought. "Let his paranoia eat him up a little." But then I imagined myself in his shoes and what would be going through my head in the same situation, so I explained why I always turned the phone face down.

At work, I used the bathroom only once a day, and during that time, I liked to have a little distraction from work so I would take my phone in with me. I always placed my phone on the toilet paper holder and since both the back of my phone and the top of the toilet holder are curved, my phone always slid down. The only way to make it stay put was to turn the face down, and I just got used to placing my phone down that way.

So now, when I place my phone face down and he's around, I make an effort to place it face up, even though my instincts want me to place it face down. When he notices, he smiles because he knows I'm making an effort. Lately, when I have sometimes placed my phone face down and haven't bothered to turn it around, he hasn't seemed to have noticed, because he now understands why I'm conditioned to place it that way.

Showing empathy

Empathy is the ability to understand or feel what another person feels in a particular situation. The Merriam-Webster dictionary defines empathy as "the feeling that you understand and share another person's experiences and emotions: the ability to share someone else's feelings".

What I have learnt from my marriage and previous relationships is that it is rarely fair. For example, I might do something or behave in a certain way and expect my partner to be fine with it, yet if the same thing were done to me, it would upset me. Early in our marriage, I established with my husband that I wouldn't get upset about a lot of things as long as he could also take whatever he dished out.

Here is what the Bible says about empathy:

> *Blessed be the God and Father of our Lord Jesus Christ, the Father of mercies and God of all comfort, who comforts us in all our affliction, so that we may be able to comfort those who are in any affliction, with the comfort with which we ourselves are comforted by God.*

> *2 Corinthians 1:3-4 (ESV)*

I tend to drift off easily; my body is present but my mind is miles away. One day, I drifted off as usual on the Tube. The train had stopped, and I looked up to check what station we were at. It was my stop and the doors had started beeping. I sprang out of my seat and out of the carriage as the doors slid shut. Then I realised in horror that I had left my purse on the train. My house keys, all my money and my train ticket were in my purse; all I had was my phone. I reported the incident to the train staff and they called ahead to the next station, but they weren't able to retrieve my purse. I gave them my details so that they could find me if and when they found it. With my heart in my shoes, I resorted to asking strangers for money to get home.

Now, every time I walk past anyone asking for help, I try to help as much as I can because I know what it feels like to be helpless and not have a way of making it back home. *I've been there.*

In the same way, I try to apply empathy in every area of my life and especially in my marriage. But I can't always relate, I haven't been through every single situation or scenario possible in the entire world; how could I possibly know what the other person is going through?

Empathising with your spouse may not be the easiest thing to do. When something bad happens to them, sometimes the first thing you think about is how it will affect *you,* especially if you feel that the unfortunate incident could have been avoided.

One day I was feeling particularly grumpy; the laundry was piling up and I found myself having to do it. I was upset because it was my husband's turn to do the laundry. In my head, I went through all the ways he was taking me for granted, expecting me to look after the kids, do my chores and still have to do his chores.

"Good morning," he called cheerily as I emptied our laundry bin onto the rug in our room to begin sorting them by colour.

"Good morning," I mumbled back.

"Are you okay?" he asked.

I straightened, ready to give him a piece of my mind. But as I prepared my argument, I realised I wasn't as innocent as I would have liked. We'd had a busy week and I had let a few things fall through the cracks as well. I put myself in his shoes. How would I feel if he attacked me about the things that I had neglected to do? I could think of at least two things he could throw back at me if I decided to make an issue of the laundry. Reluctantly, I forced my features into a smile.

"Yes, honey, I'm just tired."

Think back to a time when you could have empathised with your spouse. How did you handle the situation?

_____

_____

_____

Respect, submission and the independent woman

Respect and submission mean different things to different people.

The Merriam-Webster dictionary defines respect as "a feeling or understanding that someone or something is important, serious, etc., and should be treated in an appropriate way". Submission is defined as "the state of being obedient: the act of accepting the authority or control of someone else".

When I was younger, I was headstrong and the idea of a man ruling over me, or any woman for that matter, was something that I could not reconcile with. So the first time I read Ephesians 5:22, I didn't pay much attention to it.

> *Wives, submit yourselves unto your own husbands, as unto the Lord. For the husband is the head of the wife, even as Christ is the head of the church: and he is the saviour of the body.*
>
> *Ephesians 5:22-23*

This can't be relevant to our generation, can it? Surely, it's like the passage in 1 Corinthians 11:5:

> *But every woman who prays or prophesies with her head uncovered dishonors her head – it is the same as having her head shaved.*

It may seem that this part of the scriptures has been discarded, tossed aside as inconvenient. Why get the long, glossy Brazilian weave if I have to have it all crumpled up beneath a scarf or head tie? And just to further highlight what I felt was a gender bias, here's what it says a couple of verses down:

> *A man ought not to cover his head, since he is the image and glory of God; but woman is the glory of man.*
>
> *1 Corinthians 11:7*

I found these verses a little difficult to swallow. Before I got married, I was independent. When the song by Destiny's Child came on, I did the dance, swinging my right arm, 'disco diva' style. You know the dance, singing the lyrics with gusto – "Woah, all the ladies, independent, throw your hands up at me!" – and, boy, did I throw those hands up! I didn't need a man to complete me, and I certainly didn't need one to buy me things and lord it over me.

I said things like, "I would never let a man say that to me!" or "I would never let a man tell me what to do."

Here's an example of a woman I can relate with.

Her name was Queen Vashti. If you've never heard of Queen Vashti, it's okay, she only appeared in the Bible a few times, but in my books she is the ultimate 'Independent Woman'. Her husband was the king – not the squire, not an official, *the King of Persia,* King Xerxes – and he was a very powerful king. In fact, he was so powerful that his wife was not allowed to see him without an appointment. *I know!* Imagine if you had to make an appointment to see your husband!

The story goes that King Xerxes threw an elaborate seven-day banquet:

> *...there were couches of gold and silver on a mosaic pavement of porphyry, marble, mother-of-pearl and other costly stones. Wine was served in goblets of gold, each one different from the other, and the royal wine was abundant, in keeping with the king's liberality. By the king's command each guest was allowed to drink in his own way, for the king instructed all the wine stewards to serve each man what he wished.*

> *Esther 1:6-8*

On the seventh day, the king was in a good mood. He had just spent the last 186 days showing off his immense wealth; now it was time to show off his woman. To be fair to Queen Vashti, she was also hosting her party for the women; couldn't the king wait? So she refused to go. I can only imagine that she was thinking, "I'm not a trophy on a mantelpiece. I am extremely beautiful but there's more to me than my beauty." Some Bible translations suggest that the king, drunk and in high spirits, ordered her to be brought out wearing only her royal crown!

The king burned with anger and Queen Vashti was replaced by Esther as queen of Persia. A royal decree was issued requiring that every woman would respect her husband and every man would be ruler of his household. That last statement further highlights the fact that submission has been an issue long before my generation.

But I would have you know, that the head of every man is Christ; and the head of the woman is the man, and the head of Christ is God.

1 Corinthians 3:11 (KJV)

Submission is not a word many women want to hear when it concerns marriage but it might be the thing that will save your marriage a lot of drama. There can only be one leader. If both the husband and the wife lead then it's most likely that they will find themselves going in different directions; no one is following.

I am not asking you to submit to everything your husband says. Thoughts of Queen Vashti walking through the palace wearing nothing but her crown, her head held high but her heart and dignity slowly crumbling as more than a hundred drunken men ogle at her beauty, make me shudder inside. But I believe that there has to be a subtler way of changing your husband's heart or mind without diminishing his authority. In the movie 'My Big Fat Greek Wedding', an older woman advises a younger woman, "The man may be the head of the household; but the woman is the neck, and she can turn the head whichever way she pleases!"

I would take a page from Esther, the woman who replaced Vashti as queen. She got her husband to do what she needed by applying wisdom and asking the Holy Spirit for help.

Wives, in the same way, submit yourselves to your own husbands so that, if any of them do not believe the word, they may be won over without words by the behavior of their wives, when they see the purity and reverence of your lives.

1 Peter 3:1-2.

Respecting his masculinity

When communicating with my husband, I try to keep my focus on the end result. Do I want a fight? Or do I want to prove a point; to show that I'm right and that I'm better than he is? Do I just want peace of mind? Or do I want to know that the other person understands my point of view?

Sometimes I just walk away, when the volume of the conversation has risen and I can't see a way to achieve the result that I feel is paramount to the conversation. Sometimes it's better to walk away than for one of you to say something you will regret. Your husband will likely forgive you for walking away, it is likely that he will also forget; however, if in the heat of the argument you attack his masculinity, he might forgive but the chances are that he won't forget.

I once made such a comment during an argument. The aim of the comment wasn't to tear away at my husband's masculinity; in fact, it was in response to something equally derogatory that he had said to me. Unfortunately, in our society, throwing a jab at a woman about her financial situation will not take away her femininity, but for a man, you might as well strip him naked in the marketplace. I saw the look in his eyes and I knew that even though I hadn't meant to, I had ended up crossing an invisible line. He was silent, and I didn't need a psychologist to tell me that that was the end of the conversation. He's never said anything about it, but not long afterwards he insisted on paying all the household bills, which meant that most of his money was gone before payday was over each month. It sounded ridiculous and overly prideful to me at the time but I look back now and I respect the stance he took. And even though long gone are the days when I would even bring up finances during an argument, I wish I had just walked away that day when he made his comment. It would have upset him that I had walked away during a conversation, but he would have got over it and a simple apology would have sufficed.

A soft answer turns away wrath, but a harsh word stirs up anger.

Proverbs 15:1

Let no corrupting talk come out of your mouths, but only such as is good for building up, as fits the occasion, that it may give grace to those who hear.

Ephesians 4:29

39

Communication

My dear brothers and sisters, take note of this: Everyone should be quick to listen, slow to speak and slow to become angry.

James 1:19

Words can mean different things to different people; the way my husband says hello to me is different from how he says hello to the kids – to *each* of the kids. Body language, facial expressions, tone of voice; there are so many tells about how a person feels or thinks about you based on the way they communicate with you.

A man approaches his wife. She has a baby slung over one arm and is struggling to get her two-year-old son to stay still so that she can get him changed for bed. The little boy skips out of her grasp each time she reaches for him. With each exasperated sigh, the boy thinks it's a game that's getting even more interesting. The wife is going through the list of things she needs to do before she can even dream of going to bed. Her husband, seeing how tired and frustrated she is, smiles at her and rubs her back in a bid to make her feel better.

"Well done, hun," he says, "you're doing a great job. I don't even know how you do it."

The wife manages a tight smile. "Why doesn't he help me?" she thinks to herself.

"Anyway, I just got a call from Mike. He wants me to come over to watch the game. Is it okay if I head out?"

"Fine, have fun," she says, her face a picture of frustration and fatigue. Everything in her is willing her husband to pick up her unspoken signals. "Please stay," she pleads with her eyes.

"Great! I love you," the husband says, kissing her on the cheek and patting his son on the head before strolling out of the room whistling a happy tune, all the while thinking he has the best wife in the world.

Never assume that your spouse understands what you want or need. We want a man who's sensitive to our needs but who wants a man constantly second-guessing what would make us happy? Why don't you just tell him, not in a riddle or a parable, just plain words.

In October 2014, I received an order for a 3D character cake. The character was meant to be standing up and waving, his arms in the air with his trusty yellow truck next to him. This meant I had to build a support structure which was something I'd never done before. So, a couple of days before the cake was due, my husband accompanied me to the hardware store and we purchased the items we figured I would need. I knew I needed to build the structure in advance, but I kept putting it off. Finally, the day before the cake was due, I knew I had no choice but to face my fears. Then my husband reminded me that he had to go out that evening.

"Remember that thing I told you I had tonight? Is it still okay if I go?"

I couldn't believe it. He knew how much work I had to do; now he was going to leave me with the kids. Plus, he knew I needed help with sawing the wood, drilling holes into them and building the structure.

"If you want me to stay, I'll stay," he added.

I knew how much he wanted to go, so I replied, "No, that's fine. Have fun." Everything in me was hoping he would decide to stay, but he didn't.

That was when my troubles started. I discovered that I had the wrong type of screws. I had to get to the store quickly before it closed. We had only one car and my husband had taken it, so I took the kids round to the neighbours and called a cab to take me to the store. To my horror, the store was closed, so I headed back home where I proceeded to raid my neighbours' toolbox. I was lucky; we found one screw that would work. I needed two, but half bread would do just fine.

By midnight, I found myself calling a mutual friend who lived down the road, tears running down my face, fingers pulling at my hair. "I can't believe he did this to me!" I wailed. "Tonight of all nights! He knew I needed him to stay, but he still went."

"You silly monkey!" she said. "Why didn't you just tell him to stay?"

"Huh? But he knew..."

"Yes, of course he knew. If it were my husband, I would just say, 'Look, you're not going anywhere; I can't do this on my own.'"

"But, I don't want him to hate me and then he'll tell his friends that his wife didn't let him come out and they'll think I'm a monster."

Fast-forward a few weeks. I had an event in church I was looking forward to attending. What was even more exciting was the fact that my husband had an exam the next day. I was so ready for payback. I had brought it up all week, every single day and every chance I got, so that he would know that I was going and nothing was going to stop me.

"Bye," I sang, one foot half out the door, a big grin on my face, when my husband came up to me.

"Please stay. I can't cope with the kids tonight and I need to study."

The blood drained from my face. Surely, it couldn't be that easy. That was all? No drama, no mind games. It was so unfair and I wasn't letting go without a fight.

"But you always leave me with them even when I have exams or deliveries to make."

"What are you talking about? When have you ever asked me to stay that I didn't?" Hmm, good point. He had me there. "I just assumed you were okay and could cope," he continued.

"Fine." I admitted defeat and slunk back into the house.

I've had this conversation with my female friends over the years and nearly all of them have admitted to getting upset when their husbands don't do what they expect them to do. My next question is always, "Did you ask him to do it?" and most of the time the answer is no.

For me, I think I was afraid of what it would mean if I did ask and he said no. It would mean that I would have a genuine 'reason' (i.e. excuse) to be upset. Asking is all about free will, isn't it? The fact that I ask means that he has the right to say yes or no without the fear of condemnation.

So I started asking, "Sweetie, please could you get the kids to bed tonight?" His face would crumple into a frown and before waiting for his 'response' (excuse), I would jump in and say, "No, no, it's fine. I'll do it."

See how hard it is to get rid of passive-aggressiveness? I would spend the evening with a Cruella-like expression on my face – a face that said, "If you cross me, I will wreck you!"

But now I have mastered the art of asking. I realised, "Hey, I didn't have these kids by myself. Why do I have to do the bulk of the work?" My 'ask' has evolved to a formality, and I wait patiently for the excuse which, most of the time, never actually materialises.

It happened slowly but my husband is now more involved in the household than when I thought I had to do everything myself and rarely asked for help. Now I don't even need to ask because we've dispensed with the assumption that I am superwoman, the super-trooper, the one that can do it all.

Women need to take more time for themselves and men need to help out more. Think about it: if anything happened to you, who would have to raise the kids and look after the household?

List the things you've always wanted to ask from your spouse

1. _____

2. _____

3. _____

4. _____

5. _____

Superwoman complex

I thought I came up with the term 'superwoman complex' but there actually is such a thing. I googled it!

In a blog post titled 'Maiden, Mother, Bitch', Psychology Professor Mary Pritchard writes:

> *...superwoman complex – feeling they must do everything and do it better than anyone else has before them or they're not good enough. This complex "works" for them for a time, until they grow resentful – of their children, their spouse, their boss, the world. At that point Superwoman often takes on more of a Martyr complex. She still, begrudgingly, does it all, but she makes sure you know what she's sacrificed for you.*

I grew up in an environment where women boast about how well they can keep their family, or how much they got done before 10 am on a Saturday morning.

"I make fresh stew for my husband every day," one woman would boast. "He doesn't eat old stew; it has to be fresh."

Or, "I have to cook everything my husband eats. I won't let another woman feed my husband and my kids while I'm alive and present."

When I got married, I believed I could do it all: Business Analyst, wife, mother, cleaner, cook, shopper, tailor, baker.

My husband would suggest we get a cleaner in or order food for the week in bulk from the local Nigerian restaurant, and I would all but bite his head off. Why was he trying to take away my purpose? It was a woman's duty to do all those things and I wasn't paying someone else to do what I could do better, for free.

I look back now and it just seems ridiculous. I was stressed most of the time, I was unhappy and frustrated. I used to joke that I spent all my time on everyone else and barely had time to spare for myself. I would spend hours on my daughters' hair and less than five minutes on mine. I was noble, kind and generous but – argghh, darn those ungrateful kids! I would walk around with a grim expression on my face, resentment and anger oozing from every pore. Couldn't they see all I was sacrificing for them, so that they could have a healthy dinner, a clean house and nicely pressed clothes?

Now I know that my kids don't care about those things. So, if there's anything you can delegate around the house, let someone else do it. The chances are that you do it a lot better, it'll be hard to let go, you might even need painkillers for that migraine you get when you see what a poor job they've done, but just take deep breaths and show them how to do it the way you like. Or just let it go. Does it have to be done how you like it or can you live with how your husband likes to do it?

Trust me, your kids won't care if they miss a home-cooked meal a couple of nights a week; they might even welcome it. Don't let anyone make you feel like a bad mom or wife because you order your pot of stew from a restaurant, as long as your family eats well and are healthy.

It is okay to be selfish to a reasonable extent. Take time out for yourself; take spa breaks. I love my I-can't-deal-with-this-right-now breaks, when I just zone out and go to my happy place, where no amount of screaming and crying can reach. A note of caution, though: I only do this when my husband is around. This always jolts him into action. He knows the look; no matter what happens, unless one of the kids physically hurts themselves, nothing is taking me out of my happy place. It is invariably always followed by, "Mummy is tired right now so just leave her alone." *Ah, bliss!*

What tasks can you delegate around your home or work to save yourself from burning out?

1. _____

2. _____

3. _____

4. _____

5. _____

CHAPTER FOUR

Love Yourself

WHAT ISSUES DO YOU HAVE with yourself?

- Physical issues?
- Spiritual issues?
- Mental / educational issues?
- Financial issues?

Find a way to either deal with the issues or come to terms with the way things are. Anything you hold against yourself will come between you and your partner. If the issue is physical, create a list of ten reasons why you have that issue with your physical form and what you can do to change it. Are you up to doing whatever it takes to change it or is it not that important? If you cannot change it, can you learn to accept it?

Every time I'm unhappy with myself or going through a phase of self-hate, it always affects my relationship with my husband. How can I love him when I'm unable to love myself? In the same vein, is he treating you in a less than ideal manner? He might just be dealing with his issues or going through a self-hate phase. Be there for him as much as you can, letting him know that you're there for him. Pinpoint the source of discontent and tackle it from the root.

Whenever I feel down, under pressure or dealing with stress, I remember this Bible passage:

> *Come to me, all you who are weary and burdened, and I will give you rest. Take my yoke upon you and learn from me, for I am gentle and humble in heart, and you will find rest for your souls. For my yoke is easy and my burden is light.*
>
> *Matthew 11:28-30*

I close my eyes wherever I am and I picture a heavy weight sliding off my chest and into God's outstretched arms.

What issues do you have with yourself that is causing you discontent?

1. _____

2. _____

3. _____

4. _____

5. _____

What can you do about it?

1. _____

2. _____

3. _____

4. _____

5. _____

Let your spouse know what you're going through without assigning blame.

Daring to love yourself

When growing up, it was instilled in me to put others first. In adolescence, it was easy to ignore this. We were the ones being put first by our parents so it was okay to be selfish. Or, for example, when I was single, I could splash out on a new season Prada bag if I wanted to. My money was mine to do as I pleased. I could get up at 11 am on a Saturday morning or choose to lie in bed all day. I had no one depending on me. But now that I'm married with kids I feel like every waking moment is dedicated to catering to their needs and keeping my kids safe. Even my sleep time is not exempt. My five-year-old has eczema and the hot weather triggers a bad reaction so one night I was up at 2 am trying to calm her down. In the end, I gave up and moved her to my bed, even though doing that meant that I would end up barely hanging on to the edges of the bed and wake up feeling like a truck had rolled over me. Sometimes I feel like I have to watch them all the time to make sure they're safe. I plan my time/life around them – prayer time, workout time, sleep time – but sometimes I just have to say, "Time out! I love you but I love myself too." I need to look after myself even if it means putting them on a back burner for a while.

Comparing yourself to others

When I see a couple that look like they have it all together, I start comparing myself to them. "The wife looks amazing; she has two kids and her belly is tighter than mine was before I had children. Check out her husband, the way he looks at her, the way he's holding her like she's the most precious person in the world."

If it stopped there, it wouldn't be too bad. However, usually the trail of thought continues but in a negative vein. "Why doesn't my husband hold me like that? Why doesn't he look at me like that? Is it because I'm chubby? I bet if I looked like that he would. If only I could lose weight. If only…"

Looking at the chinks in your marriage with negative lenses creates a feeling of discontent and inadequacy. The thing you focus on becomes a yardstick for what a relationship or your marriage should be, instead of appreciating what you have, the life you've built together, the way that your husband loves you.

Comparing yourself to others is unfair to your marriage because you're yourself and not them. But you can be a better you, the best you that you can be.

The secret to happiness

What do you need to be happy? Who do you need to be for you to wake up in the morning and greet the new day with joy in your heart and lightness in your step?

The secret to your happiness lies where you place the basis of your joy.

Let's say your life is perfect (which I'm sure it is...) You're living the life you've always wanted. You have a tall, dark and handsome husband, beautiful and healthy kids, a lovely semi-detached or detached home with a large garden and a driveway, and with the latest models of your favourite cars. Your happiness is complete. You wake up in the morning, look around you and your heart swells with pride and joy. On social media, you post pictures of your idyllic life (#blessed). It's easy for anyone to see the reason behind your smile.

But what happens when you discover that your husband has been cheating on you, your kids are barely cutting it in school and you're struggling to pay your bills, with your cars and house in danger of being repossessed? In such a situation, does it then mean that you're not entitled to happiness? The joy that used to fill your heart is now locked away, deep down, in a place you struggle to reach.

Think about it this way: when you had everything, who gave you the permission to be happy? No one. It was a decision *you* made. The mind is so powerful, and I have come to realise that sometimes we need something to tie our happiness to.

What is your happiness tied to?

Your health, wealth, family, career? There is nothing wrong with that *if you have no problem gambling with your heart.* Why? None of those things are constant. In fact, the only constant is change.

Imagine Jesus as a mothership hovering in the sky of your life. When you connect to this mothership, giving it control of your life, your heart and your joy, it'll be hard for anything to steal your joy.

Nothing is under your control. I've gone through some dark emotional times, crippling debt, emotional hurt, physical pain... Those times were dark because I felt like a failure: if only I had done it this way or that way. If only I had swerved to the left when the vehicle to my right had tried to cut me off. Yet I have thought through the same situations at a different time and instead of the overwhelming darkness consuming me, I felt a lightness that I could not explain. This is because I realised that there was nothing I could have done differently to change what happened. I can't predict the future, so blaming myself for not taking an action that I could not have foreseen is only unfair to both my current self and my past self.

God is in control and since he is the only one I know who is omnipresent and omniscient, I would rather surrender control to him than fight for control.

I still have frequent moments when I tussle with God. Sometimes I get it in my head that I can do all things... in my own power. On one such day, I was really struggling. I had a few orders to get out the door and I needed to be at a market stall. I had overestimated how much I could do on my own, but I figured I would make it work. I had to; I really needed the money.

A friend came to collect her order and was shocked to see me in such a state. What she then said struck me. "Why are you struggling like you have no God?" she asked, her eyes moist with tears. She held my hands, more to stop me from dashing about than anything, and she continued, "Just relax and let God take control."

She shared her own testimony, of how her breakthrough had materialised as soon as she had let go of the tight grip she had on the reins. I indulged her.

Later that day, lugging more than half the cupcakes I had tried to sell back home, my mind was reeling on how I could still make my money back. I hauled the cakes to church the next day and tried to sell them off for a fraction of the price. The next week, I carted myself off to another outdoor market, in the freezing December cold. This time the stall did better, we had a steady throng of visitors at the cupcake stand, but unfortunately, the market had to shut down due to rain. Here I was for the second time with dozens of cupcakes I had to shift. I couldn't help the tears that trickled down at what I had gone through to make them: using the little money I had had to purchase the ingredients, staying up through the night making them so that they were fresh, while also having to deliver bespoke cake orders. I was tired and depressed, and at that point I decided I was done. I was done endangering my health and sacrificing time with my family for little returns.

A special feeling of peace and happiness enveloped me as soon as I made that decision. I completely let go and I said to myself, "Whatever will happen, will happen." The next day, I packed up the cupcakes to church, and I gave them all away. I visited close friends and I just handed them out for free.

That month was a testimony; money came in from unexpected sources and we were able to pay off our bills with extra. We even had enough to buy Christmas presents not just for our kids but for the kids of friends and relatives, something we had decided that we couldn't afford.

Share your dreams; avoid building a dream independent of your spouse.

I learnt this lesson the hard way, which, I think, is the best way to learn most lessons. I wasn't financially independent until I turned twenty-three and had my first job. Before then I had to ask someone else when I needed money for anything. Do you know how frustrating it is to have to ask for money because you're on your period and cannot afford to get sanitary products? No? Lucky you!

So, as you can imagine, when I gained financial independence, I held on tight, no going back. I felt that I had to do whatever it took never to have to ask anybody for money, even if that 'anybody' was my husband.

My husband analyses every situation and high on his list are the risks, before the gains and the benefits; he always weighs the risk and analyses our risk appetite. Between us, I think his risk appetite is low (don't tell him I told you that), whereas I have a high-risk appetite, otherwise known as a 'gambler's attitude' (I made that up so don't quote me on it). On the (frequent) occasion that I come up with a (hare-brained) idea, before I even finish, my husband flies in with his trusty cape and nerdy glasses and interrupts me (with a posh English accent that he only puts on to put me in my place), with a reel of risks and issues, and I sit there watching my idea pummelled to bits with those pointy risk flame-throwers; they don't even stand a chance. I almost always expect it now, so do you know what I do to avoid it? You've guessed it: it's so much fun when I go behind his back.

Well, it certainly is fun for a while. I do a good job of keeping it from him, however, we've built a relationship on transparency, honesty and openness and it's only a matter of time before I slip up. Plus, I'm terrible at keeping secrets from him; it's like he can read me like a book.

I made a large purchase for my bakery business. I knew it was premature and a part of me already knew what he was going to say but I really, *really* wanted it. So I made the purchase without consulting him. This wasn't a spur-of-the-moment purchase, though; I had gone through it over and over again. A few weeks before my purchase would be delivered, I received the bill of laden. My deliveries would come in twenty-one boxes. *Twenty-one!* There was no way twenty-one boxes would fit in our house!

I knew what I had to do. I had to go and confess. I braced myself for the imminent lecture.

"Honey, I ordered some cake boxes in bulk."

"Ah, so you ordered it. Nice!" he said smiling.

My jaw dropped to the floor. I blinked a few times. "What? You mean you're not upset?"

"Upset? No, why would I be upset?"

"Erm, well, it's coming in twenty-one cartons. I don't think we have space for that."

"Woah, that's a lot! Don't worry, we'll figure something out."

I had been carrying the weight and the worry on my shoulders for a long time and it felt good to be able to share it with him.

So, you see, you can never predict the way your spouse will handle a situation, and one of the things I'm learning is that you can't decide for them.

Often, when I went ahead and made decisions behind my husband's back, when he found out, my excuse was that I had already known how he would react and I wanted to avoid the reaction. But what's worse, I knew he would react negatively, yet I went ahead and did it anyway. It shows selfishness and a lack of consideration. Independent woman or not, when you get married, it is important to make decisions together and if it isn't a major decision, it is only fair to keep your spouse informed in the decisions that you make in their early stages.

It's not worth stepping out alone, and I have regretted most, if not all, of the financial decisions I have made without involving my husband.

But what if it's something you've always wanted to do but you feel that your spouse lacks the ambition or determination to push it through and so you push hard for the both of you? The downside to that is that you risk emasculating your spouse; in the end, you have to decide if it is all worth the potentially damaging effect it could have on your marriage. My advice would be to discuss it with your husband anyway. Let him know what is happening every step of the way, even as you champion the project. Keep him involved in every action, decision and every outcome, so that if a stranger walked up to him and asked him about it, he would be able to respond confidently and avoid a situation where he's in the dark about what his wife has been up to.

The 80/20 rule

The first time I heard of the 80/20 rule was in the movie 'Why Did I Get Married?' It's called Pareto's principle and according to the theory, it is likely that you will end up with 80% of what you want. However, most people tend to focus on the 20% that's missing and it makes them unhappy because, to them, they're unable to live without that 20%. Usually when it's too late, they realise they've let go of 80% for 20%. Now that isn't a fair trade...

What is that 20% that is missing from your spouse? I used to make the mistake of glorifying the 20%. "Oh, my husband doesn't do this and he doesn't do that." Now I get down on my knees and I thank God for that 80% – that is so much more than I could have asked for.

The following could be a fun exercise to try with your partner, however, approach it with sensitivity and good humour.

What is the 20% you feel is lacking in your spouse?

1. _____

2. _____

What is the 20% your spouse feels is lacking?

1. _____

2. _____

Brainstorm ideas for a walkaround to get the best of both worlds

1. _____

2. _____

Outside influences on your marriage

Don't let anyone else dictate what your marriage should look like. Don't let anyone make you unhappy about what you have. Be wary of making decisions in your marriage based on what someone else thinks. In our case, it was people asking us when we were going to buy a house and looking down at us for what we didn't have. Instead, we have chosen to focus on what we *do* have, and we are grateful every day. Often there's pressure in careless statements thrown at us from friends and family.

It's the same with having kids. Couples that have been together for years with no children are constantly bombarded with insensitive comments. If there's one thing I can guarantee, people will be insensitive. It's important to set your expectations so that such statements have no power to throw you into a tailspin of emotions.

Build up your spouse

To emasculate means to deprive someone of strength or vigour or to deprive of masculinity. Masculinity is defined as the quality of manliness. Respect should be for *who* your husband is, not *what* he has or his achievements. Many modern movies are destroying the respect men deserve by making it about all the wrong things.

People hunger for praise. What causes people to take action is whatever takes them away from pain or whatever provides pleasure. When you're constantly being told you're not good enough, soon you start believing it, so when it's time for a test or to take action, you think, "Why go through the pain of preparing, when I know I'll fail? I could be having fun (pleasure) instead." When you build your spouse up with your words and your actions both to them and to others, it is safe to say that your spouse will do everything within their power to not let you down. Before you speak to your spouse when something bothers you or they've failed at something, consider this: will what you have to say make them feel worse or will it make them want to try harder next time? Because whatever happened is in the past. You have the choice to voice your anger and frustration or communicate how you feel in such a way to reduce the likelihood that the situation will be repeated in future.

In 2012, both my husband and I found ourselves in between contracts. I watched as his optimism waned daily.

I believe that my husband has the most amazing voice in the world and before we met, he had dabbled in the music industry, doing a few shows with his childhood friend who is now an up-and-coming UK artist. I did a bit of research and I came across the 'Live and Unsigned' website. I was excited when he agreed to go for it, and we were elated and motivated when he got through the first round of auditions. Then we were faced with a dilemma. Getting through the next round of auditions would be decided by the audience. This meant that the larger the crowd we were able to gather for the event, the better his chances of getting through were. We were both closet introverts; the idea of approaching friends to buy tickets and show up for the event had us breaking out in hives.

What would people think? Would we come across as desperate? What if they didn't think we were worth the time and investment? I knew it would be easier for me to approach people on his behalf than if he were to do it himself, so I chose to let go of my fears and come out of my shell. I sent messages to as many of our friends and family as I could reach, selling them tickets and T-shirts we had designed for the show. The response was incredible: family, friends and church members turned out in droves, every one of them sporting a T-shirt with his name and face on it.

He got through that round, however, he didn't make it through the next round. After the next show, when we found out he wouldn't be getting through, I expected to find him withdrawn and moody – but he was fine. Going for the auditions had given him an opportunity to push himself and to discover what he was capable of. It was the boost of confidence he needed and it made our relationship even stronger.

He does the same for me in so many ways, every single day. As mentioned previously, I run Sophianna's Bakery, a home-based cake and pastry business, and I don't know what I would do without his support and encouragement. Whenever I have large orders, I tend to get stressed, worried that something will go wrong, but he's always there to tell me, "The cake is amazing," making those lip-smacking noises through a mouthful of cake scraps. The children even mimic him now.

Running a bakery is so stressful and I threaten to quit often but he's always there to encourage me, helping me see the big picture even though we both know that he would actually be better off without me always in the kitchen, always too tired to cook and having even less time to spend together; keeping the kids out of my way whenever I have an order; doing a 1 am Tesco run when I run out of sugar or eggs or butter; or being the delivery guy for no pay when he would rather be sleeping or watching a movie. He does all these because he knows, in the end, it makes me happy. I love baking and I enjoy the satisfaction of creating a work of art from slabs of cake. He jokes that I also love the praise and the attention when people see and taste my cakes – and he's right, but I would like to think I'm modest about it. He's the first to promote me, handing out my cards and getting people to take notice.

I don't always believe in him; sometimes I catch myself scoffing when he makes a declaration about something he wants to do which I think is ridiculous.

Recently, he decided to embark on a venture that made me nervous and he asked for my opinion. I said, "Yeah, well, if that's what you really want to do."

The next day I did some research and I sent him as many articles as I could on why it was a bad idea to do what he wanted to do. That evening we talked about it; I could see that I was getting through to him and I was silently thrilled. However, the next day, his enthusiasm was back; he had a found a way to counter everything I had thrown at him.

So, I said to him, "Whatever you decide to do, I will support you 100%." It was hard for me to say those words. I wanted to be selfish; I could see how this new venture would take up more of his time. But I also thought about how much time baking had taken me away from him and how he had always said, "I will support you 100%," and it made it easier to be less selfish.

The irony was that after that, he started having doubts about it and each time I countered his doubts with the very words he had spoken when I had raised my concerns. Being there for him meant I not only had to accept his decision, I also had to be strong for him when his faith began to wane. Unfortunately for him, it means once I'm on board with something, it is going to happen! I will keep pushing him until it does, and if he has a problem with it then tough!

In what ways can you encourage your spouse today?

1. _____

2. _____

3. _____

4. _____

5. _____

6. _____

7. _____

Chapter Five

The Things We (Married Couples) Do

Keeping score

IN ONE EPISODE OF 'RULES OF ENGAGEMENT', Audrey had kept a long list of the wrongs her husband, Jeff, had done to her throughout their marriage. *Love does not keep score of right or wrong.* The victorious feeling you expect to get from bringing up past wrongs never quite materialises. It's like a phantom; you see it but you can never grasp it. That's because your spouse is a part of you and holding on to past wrongs against him is like waging war against yourself.

Blaming

I don't know how it got so bad but it always seemed that everything that went wrong on a daily basis was my husband's fault. Because he "could have just prevented this from happening".

One morning I had missed my train – again. Down in the dumps about it, I called my husband, who happened to be working from home that day.

"Hey, hon..." I let out a deep sigh.

"What's wrong? Did you miss your train?"

"Yes, and I have to wait twenty-eight minutes for the next one. I'm going to be late again, like I have been every day this week." As ridiculous as it was, and though I wouldn't have admitted it out loud, a part of me blamed him. I had asked him if he could drop me off but he was too tired, so I had called a cab. If he had just taken me, I was confident that I would have caught the train. Even though the cab came early and I had taken a few more minutes to pack some lunch, a part of me felt like it had to be his fault. It couldn't possibly be mine, could it?

Trust me, this happened, and it happens a lot.

There are those days when you walk around the house with a face that looks like it's been stuck in a jar of rotten beans for the last hour. Your husband, looking concerned, approaches you asking what is wrong, and deep down inside you know that if you say it out loud you will sound ridiculous, so you wrinkle your nose and twist your lips into more of a grimace than a smile and you say, "Nothing. I'm fine."

I saw an advert on Facebook a few months ago. It was an animation of a lady, Brene Brown, describing how she dropped her mug one morning, spilling coffee all over her white slacks and the first thing out of her mouth was, "Damn you, Steve!" Apparently, Steve had come back home late the night before and since she couldn't go to bed until he was back, it meant she went to bed later than usual. Hence she was on her second cup of coffee which she wouldn't have been having if Steve had just come home when he was supposed to. In the animation, her husband calls while she's cleaning the mess and she tries to take it out on him but he hangs up on her because he already knows what's coming.

The first step, then, is acknowledging that the idea that your spouse is to blame in a situation where they are powerless is ridiculous. So, when I catch myself blaming my husband, I ask myself what could he have done to prevent it from happening. Also, I ask myself what *I* could have done to prevent it. After taking responsibility, the next step is to let it go – and for me, it's not an easy thing to do. I proceed to punish myself for not doing what I know I could have done to prevent the bad thing from happening. However, this is unhealthy and I'm learning to take a deep breath, face the consequences and just move on.

Think about a time when you blamed your spouse for something he had no control over.

_____

_____

_____

What could you have done differently?

Playing the victim

At some point in your relationship, you've found yourself playing the victim. It feels gratifying to release ourselves from any responsibility and to lump it on someone else, and who better to carry the cross than our husbands? It's similar to blaming, but this time, you're the victim. You constantly have negative experiences and emotions in your marriage, and it is never your fault or your responsibility.

When you catch yourself using phrases such as "he didn't let me" or "he made me", stop yourself, take a deep breath and run through the situation in your head but this time without the victim glasses.

I have to admit, it feels right to vilify my spouse. Doing this, in my head, makes me a saint; 'the blameless one'. But think about it: have you ever heard someone go on and on about how terrible someone else is; how that person is evil and how they've been the roadblock to their success and happiness? Then you ask how or what the person did and they are unable to give you a clear or direct answer. What impression did you have of the person complaining? Did you think, "Oh, this lady is a saint; she's been through so much." Or did you start running through your chore list in your head, only half-listening to the barrage of complaints, willing it to come to an end; maybe even liking or respecting that person a little less? That's the impression we give when we vilify others and make ourselves into victims.

I've heard married men complain about how their wives didn't let them pursue a business idea or a higher education. Their wives are the cages that bind them in their failure. If not for their wives and their children, they would be making millions by now. They say all this while sitting on their backsides in a pub or beer parlour, way past the hour when they should be home tucking their kids into bed! Imagine if they decided to shed that victim mentality; many would plunge into despair and depression. No, it's much safer to stick our heads in the ground and assign the blame to someone else. As I said earlier, it's so much easier to blame the spouse and so much more believable, as everyone is always quick to agree that spouses are the devil reincarnate.

There is a flip side: the fear of being the victimiser.

I went into marriage with a fear of being an 'evil woman' that would hold my husband back from achieving his dreams or following his passion. The result of such thinking is the fear of speaking your mind even when you can see that your spouse is making a mistake. I would say after the fact, "I didn't want to say anything because I didn't want you to look back and resent me." And let's face it, I could be wrong. Who knows, his idea may just have worked even though my experience had taught me otherwise.

Here is a small example but one that many of us can relate to:

I needed to scan some documents.

"Don't bother trying to use that printer," my husband said to me. "There's something wrong with it. I tried to use it yesterday and it wouldn't stop printing random stuff and wasting so much paper that I had to power it down."

"Okay, thanks," I replied, but I proceeded to insert my document into the scanner.

"I told you it's not working," he insisted. "Once you turn the machine on, it's only going to waste more paper. Why don't you just scan it at work?"

"Please, can I just try?"

"Fine, go ahead."

I turned the machine on and it scanned my document, then I turned it back off, struggling to wipe the triumphant smirk off my face.

"*What?* I was on that thing for hours yesterday," my husband said, shock written all over his face. "I'm sorry I tried to dissuade you from using it."

There are other ways this scenario could have played out. I could have chosen to listen to my husband and then have blamed him for not letting me do something I needed to do, or I could have pleaded for his patience to let me make mistakes.

If the shoe were on the other foot, I would never have dissuaded my husband from using the printer. In fact, in most instances, I wouldn't have said anything at all and then, if the printer had started malfunctioning when he turned it on, I would have said, "Oh yeah, it did that yesterday," a small guilty smile playing around my lips. And I would know what he was thinking: "Why didn't she say anything?"

I'm learning to find a balance. Now I present all the reasons why I think an idea wouldn't work and then the ultimate decision is up to my husband. The outcome of whichever path he chooses is his responsibility.

Likewise, I apply the same principle to myself.

I know that it is my husband's desire to protect me and keep me from making mistakes and so sometimes his advice might come across a bit like an order. But the decision is up to me. I can choose to listen to him and then blame him for being a hindrance to my success or I can admit that, like me, he too is fallible and that I would rather make my mistakes and hold myself responsible than resent him for 'making' me listen to his advice.

Sometimes I have gone behind his back against his advice, choosing to apologise instead of asking permission, but it feels so much better to be less cowardly and communicate how strongly I feel about my decision. One thing I find that helps to convince him is when I paint a picture of what success looks like instead of the picture of failure he's focussed on.

Passing ships in the night

We're leaving getting married until later and later in life. By the time we settle down with a life partner, we're used to our independence, the way we like to do things, the things we do. We're comfortable in our rituals built on years of looking after number one.

It's not easy to mould our lives around our spouse and it takes consciousness and maturity.

A couple may have conflicting schedules, and it is so easy to take your spouse for granted, believing that they will always be there. There will always be something more urgent to do than spending time with your spouse or someone more important to speak to than having a five-minute conversation about their day. That is, until you wake up five years down the line and struggle to recognise the person lying next to you.

It's easy to scoff and say, "That'll never happen to us." But if you don't put measures in place to ensure that you always remain each other's priority, it can sneak up on you like a bad cold.

In our first year of marriage, we thought that having a schedule for spending quality time together was a bit extreme. Surely, it would never get to the point we would need that. Now we have a list of requests from each other pinned up on a board. For example, I love taking walks so I put it on the board that I would like my husband to take walks with me. My husband's bugbear was that I was always doing something and he felt he wasn't getting my full attention, so one of his entries on the schedule was that I would spend at least half an hour with him each day, when he would have my undivided attention. We also included places we would like to visit and things we would like to do. For example, I love roller-skating but we haven't gone together since we got married; funnily enough, we met at a roller-skating centre, but life and other things (the fact that my husband is not a big fan of roller-skating) have got in the way. Usually, Wednesday night is our 'date night', and when we can't afford to go out, we spend it on the couch watching a movie.

Find a way to spend regular quality time together.

Pleasing other people

You're rushing to leave the house. The invite said 2 pm, the clock is slowly ticking towards 3 pm and you promised your friend you were going to be on time. She's counting on you to bring the games for games night.

"Come on, what are you still doing in there?" your husband yells to you as you tinker around in the bathroom.

"Keep your pants on, I'm almost ready!"

"What! We were meant to leave an hour ago. I can't believe you're still getting ready. You do this all the time. I feel like I can't even trust you to make sure we're on time for anything."

You get into an argument and eventually everyone gets into the car. You could cut the tension in the vehicle with a knife, and you arrive at the venue fuming. Then your friend greets you at the door with a broad smile.

"Hello, you're the first ones here!"

This used to happen a lot. Every time we were running late to an event, there would be an argument, finger-pointing.

"It's your fault."

"No, it's your fault."

And then we would get there only to realise that it wasn't a big deal that we were late.

Look, things happen! People are late for different reasons; maybe it was his fault, maybe it was yours, and next week no one will care or even remember. At the end of the day, you and your spouse will have to face one another. Your spouse is more important than the people you're trying to please. Be careful that you don't hurt their feelings for the sake of those people.

Judging other people's marriages

"Hmm, poor guy, did you hear the way she spoke to him? If she can do that here, I shudder to think how she talks to him at home."

Or...

"She's a terrible wife, always travelling, leaving her husband alone to look after the kids."

Criticizing other people's marriages can make you feel good about yours; you've compared your marriage with theirs using only one yardstick and yours comes out trumps. The gratification you get is counterproductive. What if the way you judge others is what is holding you back from achieving anything?

For example, you get an offer for a job with excellent pay and benefits but it includes some travel. You're afraid to take the job because you're worried that people will judge you the way you've always judged others.

Someone once called me a wicked woman for leaving my kids with my husband for four days to travel to Nigeria for my brother's wedding. I wasn't sure if he was joking or serious, and my jaw dropped. My first instinct was to pity his wife, the fact that she could never leave her kids with him if she were in a similar situation where she couldn't take the kids with her – but I stopped myself. I can't claim to understand him or his perceptions, but I would have appreciated it if he had kept them to himself.

You hear people tell you what a married woman should and shouldn't do, and sometimes I marvel. Just because you have a particular perception of marriage, don't try to push that on someone else. Who is to say that their marriage isn't perfect for them? Your judgements are more of a reflection of who you are and how you think than they are about the other person or couple.

There are times when I have stopped to take a closer look at myself in the middle of a judgemental party about someone else or their relationship, and what I have noticed is that the thing I tend to focus on is the thing I'm struggling with myself.

> *Why do you look at the speck of sawdust in your brother's eye and pay no attention to the plank in your own eye?*
>
> *Matthew 7:3*

I believe that judging others creates a burden on us that can lead to dissatisfaction with our relationship, or self-hate. It can also lead to a sort of paralysis or inability to take action out of fear that we will be judged similarly.

CHAPTER SIX

Misconceptions I Had About Marriage

Misconception no. 1: That love is enough

FOR SOME TIME AFTER WE got married, I didn't work on my marriage. In fact, I barely focussed on it. How could I? I had just got married, had a baby, did all the cooking and cleaning and still had to leave the house for over ten hours a day to go to work. As long as my husband was alive and breathing, that was good enough for me.

What about a *good* marriage? That depends on what your definition of a good marriage is. I've taken mine from the Bible.

> *Husbands, love your wives, as Christ loved the church and gave himself up for her, that he might sanctify her, having cleansed her by the washing of water with the word, so that he might present the church to himself in splendour, without spot or wrinkle or any such thing, that she might be holy and without blemish. In the same way husbands should love their wives as their own bodies. He who loves his wife loves himself. For no one ever hated his own flesh, but nourishes and cherishes it, just as Christ does the church, because we are members of his body. "Therefore a man shall leave his father and mother and hold fast to his wife, and the two shall become one flesh." This mystery is profound, and I am saying that it refers to Christ and the church. However, let each one of you love his wife as himself, and let the wife see that she respects her husband.*
>
> *Ephesians 5:25-33 (ESV)*

But how should we love our spouse? I found the answer to that question in 1 Corinthians 13:4-7

> *Love is patient and kind; love does not envy or boast; it is not arrogant or rude. It does not insist on its own way; it is not irritable or resentful; it does not rejoice at wrongdoing, but rejoices with the truth. Love bears all things, believes all things, hopes all things, endures all things.*

ESV

I'll put my hands up; based on this definition, loving my husband is hard work. It means I have to be patient and kind, even when I think he's doing something the wrong way. It means I shouldn't always insist on having my way; I can consider *his* way of doing things sometimes! Love is not irritable or resentful – I'm working on that, but it might be the toughest one yet.

Love in itself is sufficient for a marriage to succeed; however, in a relationship where the two of you have to share the same space, *love might not be enough.* I believe that the best marriages are the ones in which both people change their old ways to merge as one, different but complementing each other. You are only as strong as the weakest link, holding each other up, having each other's backs in any situation.

A few weeks after our wedding, we threw a small get-together for my birthday. A debate started, the topic of which I cannot recall. My husband made a statement which I immediately opposed and my mom, who was visiting at the time, gave me a look but said nothing.

After the party, she said to me, "Always put up a united front with your husband in public. If you disagree with something he says, just be silent." I looked at her like she had grown two heads.

"Mom," I said, "my generation is different from yours. Are you saying I shouldn't have differences of opinion with my husband?" It didn't make sense to me.

Now I think I understand where she was coming from. A man wants to feel respected, and in a public setting the last person he expects to challenge his knowledge and intelligence is the one person who, in the traditional sense, is supposed to be submitted to him.

One day my husband said something that struck a nerve. We were having a discussion and he noted, "You never take my side. It's almost like it would kill you to agree with me for once."

My response was, "Yes, but if you feel that way, why don't you take *my* side then?"

Now, instead of saying, "I completely disagree! You are wrong and I am right because..." I'm learning to say, "That's an interesting point and I'm sure it's valid, but would you consider this perspective...?" In this manner, I'm not claiming his opinion is not valid but I'm asking him to consider an alternative view.

Misconception no. 2: That all is fair in love and war

Do not repay evil with evil or insult with insult. On the contrary, repay evil with blessing, because to this you were called so that you may inherit a blessing. For, "Whoever would love life and see good days must keep their tongue from evil and their lips from deceitful speech. They must turn from evil and do good; they must seek peace and pursue it."

Peter 3:9-11

When you get into an argument or when you feel any resentment towards your spouse, you can try this exercise.

Think about what upset you. Try to verbalise it. Write it down; read it to yourself. Decide what action to take:

1. Let it go.
Perhaps it was a minor misunderstanding. Maybe you've looked at it from his perspective and you've come to realise that you overreacted or that he didn't mean to hurt you. Speak to him about it, explain why what he did upset you; not in a confrontational manner but in a calm manner.

2. Tackle it.
What action could you take? Whatever decision you make, take it to God. Trust in him to have the best interests for your marriage.

Before we got married, our fights were relatively mild; I had captured the art of walking away to a T. We didn't have to address it if I didn't want to. However, when you're living in a small two-bedroom apartment, there's nowhere to run. I think back to our fights and I shudder to think of the amount of hate and anger that spewed forth in our desires to prove to the other person that they were the more flawed one.

Remember that we are all flawed.

Jesus addresses our hypocritical nature in Matthew 7:3-5:

> *Why do you look at the speck of sawdust in your brother's eye and pay no attention to the plank in your own eye? How can you say to your brother, 'Let me take the speck out of your eye,' when all the time there is a plank in your own eye? You hypocrite, first take the plank out of your own eye, and then you will see clearly to remove the speck from your brother's eye.*

No one is faultless.

Let me give an example of a typical scenario.

You did something he didn't like. You had no idea it would be an issue so you weren't doing it to hurt him on purpose. He confronts you about it in an accusatory manner and as he speaks, you're slowly getting riled up. He doesn't understand why you're getting angry since it was you that upset him in the first place. And then you go around in circles, throwing razor-sharp words, with the intent to see who can cut the deepest. Voices are rising higher and higher, tempers are flaring and all you can see is red. Your blood is at boiling point and then you say *those words* – words that seem fair in the light of your situation but even you know that you've crossed the line. Those words could be anything, but they will carry on, long after the argument has been resolved, long after it's been forgotten; the words will remain, hanging in the air between you. He'll always know that deep down that's what you think of him. His behaviour towards you changes. You don't know why; you've cried about it to anyone who will listen. Why does he treat you differently, why won't he be better? You've forgotten those words; surely, he understands that you didn't mean them, that you only uttered them because you were angry? But he didn't forget. Those words play in his head over and over again – if that's what you think of him, then how can he trust you?

Galatians 5:15 warns us against tearing each other apart.

> *But if you keep attacking each other like wild animals, you had better watch out or you will destroy yourselves.*

Then it offers a solution in the next verse.

If you are guided by the Spirit, you won't obey your selfish desires.

There's more at stake in a marriage and so the fights mean more.

When you're arguing, fight fairly. Remember that you still have to share a roof. Avoid name-calling or making accusations; stick to the facts. Think about what your fight will achieve. Is it to prove that you are right? Or that you are better than your spouse?

Exercising self-control is important. The last thing you want is to look back and be disgusted with your behaviour during the argument.

I realised that, more often than not, the basis for my anger was unfounded, especially if I saw the issue from the other person's point of view. I could easily have made the same mistakes they made.

I hate it when my husband and I fight, so I try to avoid it as much as possible. He always wants to know if I'm angry or upset and it's in his nature to hash things out, while I would much rather sweep things under the rug. So, whenever I'm upset and he wants to talk about it, I ask him as peacefully as I can to allow me to calm down first. Whenever I speak when I'm upset, my voice rises, and then his voice rises, and then we forget why we're arguing and it turns into a full-blown fight. Instead, then, I find a quiet place to calm down. In my head, I'm thinking of the best approach to address the issue without sounding like I'm accusing him of something. I think of what I want the outcome of our discussion to be and I focus on that.

Do I want to be right? Do I want to teach him a lesson? Or do I want us to be okay, smiling and holding each other in love?

Sometimes I find it helps to say a quiet prayer.

The last time we were about to argue, I closed my eyes and muttered under my breath, "I don't have to be right," over and over again until I felt that I was in control again.

I'm not perfect and neither is he; we're learning each day to love one another in spite of our imperfections.

You and your spouse are one. A body divided against itself will not stand. And when you fight, let go of pride. A proud heart is an abomination to the Lord.

Usually, my husband is the first to apologise when we argue, no matter whose fault the argument is. He says, "It's for the sake of peace." I remember the look of shock on his face the first time I apologised after an argument. I'm slowly learning to let go of pride; in the end, we are both better off when peace reigns.

When one person is angry, the other person should exercise self-control until the angry person calms down.

Misconception no. 3: That you will have sex less often

You might not notice anything changes to your sex life in the first few years of marriage, before the kids come, but when the little munchkins start popping out, it can be hard to find the energy even to *want* to have sex.

Sex should not be the focus of your relationship. You probably know that, and I did too but it didn't really sink in for me. See, I had my first child before we got married, two weeks before to be precise, so there was no honeymoon period for us; we were smack bang in the middle of a crisis. It was a trying time and I remember not being remotely in the mood. After all, having sex was what had placed us in our predicament in the first place. But I was afraid, too; I worried that not having sex meant there was something wrong with our relationship.

There will be high and low seasons, but it should not determine the state of your relationship with your spouse or be used as a scale measuring the love in, or the solidarity of, your marriage. I've come to realise that my mood for sex has nothing to do with my feelings for my husband.

> *The husband should give to his wife her conjugal rights, and likewise the wife to her husband. For the wife does not have authority over her own body, but the husband does. Like-wise the husband does not have authority over his own body, but the wife does. Do not deprive one another, except perhaps by agreement for a limited time, that you may devote yourselves to prayer; but then come together again, <u>so that Satan may not tempt you because of your lack of self-control</u>.*
>
> *1 Corinthians 7:3-5 (ESV, emphasis added)*

I have a friend who says she set herself a challenge to have more sex with her husband. So she set up a money jar by her bed and each time they had sex, she put a coin in the jar. Her aim was to make sure that each year the money jar had more in it than the year before.

Another friend says she has sex with her husband every night as much as they can. I don't know how that is possible! They make sure they resolve any arguments they might have because they know that once it's bedtime, they have to be together, and they would like it to be without any awkwardness.

Find a way that works for you. If you have to schedule it in, then why not? Set yourselves a challenge, or take it in turns to initiate it, like a roster.

Misconception no. 4: That you will never find another man attractive

Everyone at one point in their lives will be tempted.

> *"No temptation has overtaken you except what is common to mankind. And God is faithful; he will not let you be tempted beyond what you can bear. But when you are tempted, he will also provide a way out so that you can endure it."*
>
> *1 Corinthians 10:13*

> *Marriage should be honored by all, and the marriage bed kept pure, for God will judge the adulterer and all the sexually immoral.*
>
> *Hebrews 13:4*

In an ideal world, you meet the man of your dreams, settle down and get married. Your hormones switch off and you never find another man attractive for the rest of your life. Unfortunately, we do not live in an ideal world and it is a mistake to assume that you are immune to attractions to anyone other than your spouse.

You might say, "I love my husband so much, there's no way I would cheat on him." And that is great. I applaud that. I used to think like that, too. I would say, "I have a lot of self-control. I will never be unfaithful." And while I am not saying that I cheated on my husband, I have come to accept that I am human.

That is a good start, admitting that you are human and, therefore, are not infallible. The next step is to protect yourself and your marriage by removing yourself from any compromising situations.

For fun, I googled the phrase 'compromising situation' and this was the first listing:

> *"Compromising" usually used as "found in a compromising position" or (especially if referring to a sexual act) "in flagrante delicto" are typically euphemistic newspaper terms meaning "caught with your pants down" i.e. doing something romantic/sexual with someone other than your long term partner.[1]*

It was in response to a question on Quora.

Exchanging texts and phone calls with the opposite sex that have gone beyond pleasantries and communicating information is veering into dangerous territory.

Years ago, I was talking to my friend Bimpe about the fact I don't have any male friends, which would have been unthinkable to me before I got married. It felt like all my male friends had slunk away as soon as I had got married; strangely, I didn't miss any of those relationships. They weren't beneficial to me and it was nice not to have to deal with any drama or jealousy within my marriage.

"My husband is close friends with a female work colleague. They talk on the phone almost every day, and sometimes those conversations go on for hours," she blurted out.

"How do you feel about it?" I asked.

"I hate it. But he said there's no reason to be jealous; they're just friends."

I wish I had had some advice that would have helped her back then. Unfortunately, what I said was, "Yeah, that's what a guy I once dated said, but as soon as we broke up, they started dating," which further deepened her suspicions and insecurity.

It is possible that the relationship is completely innocent, but if it makes your spouse uncomfortable, is it worth it? Is that relationship worth your marriage?

For me, the answer was and still is no. If one phone call to a male friend means five hours of discomfort in my home, you can bet that I will go as far as blocking the number from my phone. I thank God that my husband and I have the same stance.

---

[1] *https://www.quora.com/What-does-in-a-compromised-position-mean#!n=12*

Spending a lot of time alone with the opposite sex in an enclosed environment is a recipe for disaster. What if you're not attracted to the person – surely it shouldn't be a problem then? But what if by spending time together, you begin to open yourself up to this person? You start building common ground and physical attraction may well follow. I'm not saying that it will *always* happen, just that it *can* happen.

Speak to people who have cheated on their partners and most of them will admit that, "It just happened." That is all it takes to ruin a marriage and the trust you've built with your spouse: the 'it' that just happened.

Another common theme is, "I don't know what came over me." By this, someone means that they lost all control and their lustful desires took over. In some cases, remorse and guilt follow immediately. They've thrown away the lives they've built with their partners and the security of their children on a callous mistake.

You can protect yourself by being honest with yourself. Be aware when you feel an attraction to someone else bubbling under the surface. Some people say you should discuss it with your spouse. I don't know. Only you know your spouse enough to determine if this is an appropriate action.

I don't think I would want to know that my husband has feelings for someone he works with, unless he plans to leave that job. I know myself and I am honest about it. That is not to say that I don't trust him. I do. But I also know that he is only human. And so every day when he goes in to work, I would experience pangs of anxiety, checking up on him constantly, wondering what he is doing. Is he talking to her, or spending more time with her? Do they sit together at lunchtime? Are they talking about me? Is he telling me only half of the story? What time will he be home? Shouldn't he be home by now? It only takes twenty minutes to get home and it's already 5.23 pm. Insecurity does crazy things to your mind.

What would I do if I found myself in a situation where I were attracted to someone other than my husband? I would pray about it. You might have to choose between your job and your marriage. If possible, get transferred to another team or building.

Don't be complacent or nonchalant about it. Don't say, "I have to work with him. It's my job; what can I do?" At least try something. Cut off all unnecessary contact. If the two of you usually have meetings together, make sure there's a third person present at the meeting. Find a way to include another department or individual in your conversations.

It might be tempting to want to see the other person, but if you give in to temptation, bring up an image of your spouse in your mind and what it would do to them if you ever gave in to a little harmless flirtation. Just as a tiny spark has the potential to erupt into a fire that consumes everything in its path, a little flirtation can escalate into a full-blown affair. Hearts are broken, families are torn apart. People who look up to your marriage have lost a role model.

> *But I tell you that anyone who looks at a woman lustfully has already committed adultery with her in his heart.*
>
> *Matthew 5:28*

Do everything in your power to purge indecent thoughts of the other person from your mind. However, do not rely on your own strength. Seek God, ask for his help. If you can speak to your spouse, do. Tell them you need their help. Seek counsel from elders and, most importantly, see counsel from the Bible.

> *Finally, brothers, whatever is true, whatever is honourable, whatever is just, whatever is pure, whatever is lovely, whatever is commendable, if there is any excellence, if there is anything worthy of praise, think about these things.*
>
> *Philippians 4:8 (ESV)*

CHAPTER SEVEN

Be Careful What You Say About Your Spouse

IT'S EASY TO GET CARRIED AWAY when you're angry with your spouse. It's easy to criticise and to judge. I have seen women, married for years, their relationships look perfect on the outside, but they still call their husbands names when they're angry. Sometimes it's hard for us as humans to restrain our anger and just let it go. However, be careful what you say to your friends. It might seem harmless, but what you are voicing in frustration may well be amplified in their minds way out of proportion. Also, remember that not everyone you speak to is truly your friend or has your very best interests at heart.

To keep our anger in check, it is worth remembering that relationships are not always equal and cannot be expected to be so all the time. In many African marriages, marriage is skewed in favour of the man. Sometimes the man can get away with murder – but on another occasion the woman might be able to get away with it, leaving the man at a disadvantage.

You may have heard the saying, "If you have nothing good to say, say nothing at all." When ladies congregate to talk about their spouses, more often than not it is not in a flattering light. Don't believe me? Think back to the last time you heard two or more ladies talking about their husbands in a flattering light; how long did that conversation last? I can boast about my husband all day long, but no one wants to listen to me boast; it's boring!

We complain to our friends about 'what he did' and 'what he didn't do'. It seems like husbands have caught the short end of the stick when it comes to being able to do anything right (i.e. exactly the way we want them to). Remember, though, that unless your friend is very close or a relative of your husband, whatever you say about him is the way the hearer will view him. So, if you paint him as a monster, guess what? Your friend will be worried for you, believing your life is in danger. This opens the door to them being disrespectful, because they've lost any respect they may have had for your husband. The last thing you want to have to do is choose between your husband and your friend, and sometimes that is the result of such seemingly innocent conversations.

For example, Tolu invited her friend Funke over. She noticed her husband Timi was acting strange and it made her uncomfortable. He looked angry and Tolu couldn't understand why. As soon as Funke left, Tolu rounded on Timi, her nose flaring.

"What is wrong with you? Couldn't you just be nice for once? Can't I have friends over anymore?" The tone of her voice rose as she spoke; she tapped her foot and gestured wildly with her hands, the way she always did when she was upset with him.

"How can you even ask me? Did you not see that your friend was disrespectful to me, in my own house?"

"Why? What did she do? I was sitting here and I didn't see her do anything disrespectful," she screamed into his face.

"I mean, I walked in and she couldn't even say hello."

Tolu hissed. "So – because she didn't say hello?"

"Not just that. Her whole attitude. She even eyed me. Did you not see that?"

"I'm sure you imagined it. Or maybe she had something in her eye." Tolu rubbed her neck as she looked anywhere but at her husband.

"What have you been saying to her? Did you tell her about the fight we had? Because that's the only reason I can think of that would make her act like that."

"Well…" Tolu twirled her ring around her finger as she cast her mind back two days before. She recalled the words she had spoken to her friend.

"Selfish, good-for-nothing man… He can't even get a job. How dare he be upset when I spend my money on the things that I want?"

"Really? Some men are just useless," Funke had said, empathising with her friend. "So, does he want to spend the money for you?"

Now Tolu looked up at Timi and said the only thing she could say. "No, of course not. I didn't say anything to her."

"Well, she's not welcome here anymore."

"*What?* How can you do that to me?"

You and your spouse are two different individuals, living in the same space and having to make decisions together. The chances are that you will not agree on most of those decisions and feelings of resentment can creep in. Longing for the 'good old days' when you could have your own way without having to discuss it with anyone can leave you looking for an out. But before you say anything about your spouse, take a moment to think: if your spouse were eavesdropping on every conversation you've had about him, would you still be together?

Have someone you can talk to; someone you trust and preferably someone who is in a stable marriage that you admire, someone you can depend on to put you on the right track instead of taking your side each time you discuss anything pertaining to your marriage.

Focus on the good in your relationship

"So, what is it that you think I do well? What do you appreciate about me?" my husband asked one evening.

It was date night and we were sat opposite each other, savouring the delicious meal and absence of our kids. He was smiling broadly, in what I can only assume was an anticipation to a barrage of compliments. I watched as his lips slowly inched into a grim line as I um-ed and ah-ed. It took me more than ten minutes to come up with two things that I appreciated about him.

With a wary look on his face he asked, "…and what things do you think I need to improve on?"

I smiled at him, ready and aimed to begin. This was the territory I was comfortable in.

He interrupted me after two minutes. "How come it's so easy for you to list what I do wrong and it's so hard to list what I do right?"

"I'm sorry, hon, I just can't remember. I'm sure there are more things you do really well," I said, not really feeling sorry.

He started listing the thing he appreciated about me, things that I would never have thought about and, as he spoke, I thought about some of the things he did on a daily basis that I had overlooked but would miss if he stopped doing them; like taking out the trash, straightening up after me when I'm rushing around, having to go without food or distracting the kids when I've got cake orders, going out in the middle of the night to Tesco because I've run out of unsalted butter or icing sugar for a cake due the next day, giving me a massage when I'm tired, always, constantly asking if I'm okay, always being the first to say sorry, even when we both know I'm being irrational. I could go on and on... I mean, I do a lot of things in the house, and if it were a competition I would clearly be the winner, but it's *not* a contest. We both have our strengths and weaknesses, and we should work to complement one another.

"What do I need to improve on?" I asked, already feeling awesome with the way he had made me sound like a superwoman.

"Um... I can't think of anything."

"Really?" I asked, feeling bad now for making him out to be so terrible

"Yeah... um... maybe just tidy up your side of the room."

It's a lot easier to focus on what is wrong about a relationship than to focus on what is great about it. Just remember, no relationship is perfect; every marriage will go through rough patches.

Appreciate the 'little things' your spouse does. Let them know how much you appreciate them for doing those things because it's easy for the negative emotions to overshadow the positive. I'm learning to change my focus.

Write down the things your spouse does that you appreciate.

1. _____

2. _____

3. _____

4. _____

5. _____

Keeping a journal

Is there's one thing I wish I had done before I got married, it's that I wish I had kept a journal.

I used to keep one when I was a teenager but for some reason I stopped. When I now read my entries, they're so precious to me. It feels like I'm reading a stranger's words. Your perception will change over time and when you have been married for a while, sometimes you begin to forget what it was like when you met your spouse: how they made you feel; the things you did to get them to notice you; the dates you went on. All these memories fade with time. How amazing would it be when you're going through a rough patch to have a reminder of the way it was when you fell in love? However, it's not too late to start now. Keeping a journal of your relationship will help you focus on it. There are some days when I feel like we're ships passing in the night; we both have different schedules and at the end of the day we both want to kick back and watch TV, but unfortunately, we both have different viewing interests and it takes effort and determination to spend time together. Keeping a journal will also help you track if you've spent dangerously little time together, alerting you to make a change before the situation becomes disastrous.

Listening

I continually find myself explaining to my husband that when I tell him about my day or about something that's bothering me, I'm not looking for a solution, lecture or a pep talk; I just need him to listen. However, sometimes I get cut off in the middle of my moan because he believes he has 'cracked the code' and doesn't even need me to complete what I'm saying.

I was out of the country for a few days and his mom came over to help with the kids. The second night into my trip he called to apologise. "I'm sorry," he said. "I now understand how you feel when you talk to me. My mom is constantly offering me advice and solutions, and it's driving me crazy!"

I burst out laughing. "So, will you stop doing it?"

"I can't promise anything, but I'll make more of an effort. I'm not going to watch you making a mistake and just say nothing."

"Yes, but you can try to let me come to the solution by myself, instead of immediately jumping in to fix all my problems."

"Hmm... I *can* do that."

Most times when I moan and whinge about an issue, I know what to do to fix it. When my husband blurts out a solution, I feel like he's indirectly saying I'm too stupid to have thought of such a simple solution, and it kills my thunder. My ideal conversation would go like this:

"I'm so frustrated with _____ down at the _____..." The monologue continues for ___ minutes with no interruption.

My husband pays attention, taking care to show that he is fully present, nodding and inserting hmm's and ah's in all the right places, ignoring his phone when it rings or a text comes in until I finish speaking.

He then pauses to make sure I am actually done and not just pausing for breath. (This has never happened – ever!) "Oh no, that's _____ [insert any of the following: not fair, ridiculous, outrageous etc.]"

"I know..."

"What are you going to do?" (Notice how this statement is so much different from, "Here's what you should do..." or, "Why don't you just...")

"Maybe I'll _____ [insert my solution here]."

"That's an excellent idea."

At the end of the conversation I can guarantee that I feel energised. We have come to the solution to my problem and I feel valid and smart – the opposite of how I feel when I get told what I should do or what I should have done.

I have my faults with listening as well. While my husband is a problem-fixer and the source of all solutions, I tend to analyse the situation. I would think, there must be a reason why so-and-so did what he did, or why my husband wasn't chosen to do something he wanted to do even though he was qualified for it; then I would proceed to list all the possible reasons. Sometimes my husband was looking for a solution or ideas on how to fix the problem, but because I found it frustrating when he gave me these kinds of solutions, I responded to him in the way I wished he would interact with me. What this meant was that our 'listening' relationship was less than ideal. We're not there yet but I have begun to understand that his solutions and fixes are coming from a good place and he now knows that I'm programmed to treat people how I would like to be treated and might not immediately jump in to save the day! He needs to explicitly ask for my opinion or ideas to spur me into action.

There is power in the tongue

I remember the first time I heard the phrase, "An angel of the Lord passed by and everything you've just said will come to pass." I must have been seven years old at the time and was at the dining table with some of my siblings and cousins. Our conversation was loud and rowdy, but at one point everyone fell quiet. The silence was deafening and probably lasted for a second. Then one of my cousins whispered as if in awe, "An angel of the Lord passed by and everything you've just said will come to pass." I felt goosebumps; it was so spooky that I never forgot it. So, growing up, I became wary of an angel passing by and putting a stamp on my words, watching my tongue, in case something bad happened. Sometimes when I had been careless or daring, I would say a prayer inwardly, "Please don't let it happen. Please don't let it happen."

> *Death and life are in the power of the tongue, and those who love it will eat its fruits.*
>
> *Proverbs 18:21*

Knowing that there are heavenly witnesses to what we say can be a good thing, and should not always be something to fear. Instead of just guarding my tongue against evil, I can use it to give life. Now I use this power to speak life into my marriage, into my husband and into my kids.

The words that you speak to your spouse, to his face and behind his back, carry with them the power of life and death. Sometimes you just want to vent to a friend about the frustrations of married life and sometimes it is enjoyable to just let it rip – I know, I have been there – but it always leaves a bitter taste in your mouth.

If this is you, I can promise you that it'll be hard at first. You've done it for so long that your mind is programmed to criticise. But when you're tempted, stop and think: "What if every word you uttered against your husband became a reality? Would you still curse him or would you bless him?"

When I feel a bitter word creeping up my throat, I try to swallow it down, thinking of something positive to say instead.

Write down all the positive you would like to speak into your spouse's life.

1. _____

2. _____

3. _____

4. _____

5. _____

CHAPTER EIGHT

When You Feel Trapped in Marriage

ALWAYS BE IN A POSITION to be able to leave. The last thing you want is not to be able to leave a terrifying situation that puts you and your children in danger, for fear of how you'll survive. The person you married may have been the best when you got married, but human beings change.

In the movie 'This Christmas', Regina King's character works in her mom's laundry business and we understand that she doesn't earn a lot of money. Her husband is the primary breadwinner and from the beginning of the movie, we can already see that something is not right in the marriage. He speaks down to her and bullies her. All he has to do is clear his throat and she jumps to attention. Her sister, who cannot stand him, finds out that he's having an affair and when she confronts Regina King's character about it, she utters two words: "I know."

Her sister's jaw drops.

But Regina King is not done; she continues, "Look at me. What do I have going for myself? Where will I start from? Who will have me?"

She didn't say, "I love him so much and I want this marriage to work out." Watching it, I saw the resentment bubbling under the surface and, most of all, the insecurity and lack of self-esteem.

I am an advocate that couples should fight for their marriages. I love the movie 'War Room', in which a woman, knowing that her marriage is dangling over the edge, goes on a mission to save her marriage by fighting on her knees (in prayer). However, not once during that movie did I get the sense that she was afraid to leave her husband. In fact, I believe that knowing you can leave and choosing to stay is immensely powerful. Fear does dangerous things to the mind.

I know what it feels like to want to leave a relationship but be in fear of the possible consequences. Where would you live? How will you feed? I was a student then, living in a house that my boyfriend at the time had got for me. My parents were unaware; I lied to them that I had got a job, but getting a job and maintaining it would have been impossible as the course I was studying meant that I travelled often.

I prayed then that I would never be in a situation where I would have to depend on a man. Do whatever you can do: learn a new skill; find a passion. The Internet age has made it easier than ever to start a business from home while looking after kids.

I started my cake business when I was out of work for six months. It was a skill I had developed over five years. Before I started the business, my husband used to get upset that I refused to ask him for money and that I worried constantly about how I would pay my bills.

"You make it seem like this is all on you. I'm working; I can help," he would say.

Then my mind would flash back to the time I had had to wait for my boyfriend to come over so that he could give me money for sanitary towels, and I would shake my head.

I could walk away from my marriage today and know without any doubt that I would be able to take care of myself and my kids – but I choose to stay, and to me that is essential.

Finances

Have you had the money conversation yet?

Do you know how much he earns? Or even what he does for a living? Is he comfortable showing you his bank account? Or does he hide financial details from you?

Is he in debt? How much does he owe? What is his spending style? Does he use his credit card to purchase frivolous items and then struggle to pay his rent? Does he take you out on a shopping spree even though you know he doesn't have a job?

Ask all the financial questions you can as soon as you decide to get married and be prepared to come clean about your financial situation as well. Many marriages have broken up because of finances; at least you'll know what you're getting yourself into.

With everything that was going on around the time my husband and I got married, it never occurred to us to have the money talk. We were barely scraping by, staggering under the weight of rent, childcare and food bills, not to speak of all the other taxes we were unprepared for. Who knew you had to pay Council Tax and Corporation Tax?!

We kept our accounts separate, but we've always been of the mindset that we share everything. Even in those early years of our marriage, I was happy to give him the last penny I had if he needed it.

Financially, my husband and I have been through some very challenging times, but we've also enjoyed some good times too. I'll be the first to admit that even though money isn't a priority in our marriage, lack of money can put a strain on a relationship. People become more sensitive as insecurities set in; any reference to money or lack of it can be misconstrued as an insult. In some cases, we had to pull our kids out of nursery or cancel their childcare arrangements, adding another stressful factor into the equation. It is for this reason that I always implore my single friends not to let money be a determining factor in the choice of a mate. Money is fickle; even Job, an extremely wealthy man, lost all his wealth in less than a week. Money can be lost and money can be regained, but love should be constant.

Regarding savings, I read an article a while back which advised couples to save half of what they earn. It suggested that a couple should only spend one person's salary, leaving the other salary untouched. While I felt that this advice was sound, I realise that it isn't realistic for many households.

Whatever you do, it is important to pay off your debts.

> *Pay to all what is owed to them: taxes to whom taxes are owed, revenue to whom revenue is owed, respect to whom respect is owed, honor to whom honor is owed. Owe no one anything, except to love each other, for the one who loves another has fulfilled the law.*
>
> *Romans 13:7-8 (ESV)*

> *The wicked borrows but does not pay back, but the righteous is generous and gives...*
>
> *Psalm 37:21 (ESV)*

Ensure that your bills are paid on time, and if you're worried that you won't be able to meet a particularly monthly bill, it is better to call up the organisation to discuss your financial difficulties. You'll be amazed how understanding they can be. As long as the lender knows that you're willing to pay but are unable to due to circumstances beyond your control, more often than not they are happy to work out a repayment plan with you. It benefits them to do this, as the alternative for them is to sell your debt to a debt collection agency who will buy your debt at a fraction of the cost, losing your lender money. Even HMRC are lenient as long as you are transparent about your difficulties.

My husband and I have maintained our separate accounts but we also have a joint one into which we both put an equal amount of money every month. We do this to avoid any disputes about who owns what or who contributes more. Even though we both know that whatever we have belongs to both of us, there's no telling how we might feel about it in the future.

One thing we try to do at least once a year is to review where we are financially. My husband is more adept at spreadsheets so he creates them, but you can also use one of the Microsoft templates. We make a list of all our monthly outgoings and compare it against our income. This allows us to decide how much we can put into the joint account each month. If you can, include your holidays in the plan as well. Include birthdays and anniversary and Christmas planning. Review forecast versus actuals at least quarterly. There are some very good budgeting apps out there if you're 'allergic' to spreadsheets. One example is 'Money'. I like it because of the pretty pictures (!) and the fact that I can update it as I go, allowing me to see how much I have left and to budget appropriately.

YOUR INITIAL MONEY CONVERSATION GUIDELINE

- Debt situation: How much is owed and to whom?
- Discuss your financial commitments, for example, mortgage, sibling responsibility, etc.
- Monthly disposable income.
- Realistic monthly savings
- How will bills be paid? From a joint account or will bills be split?

- How will our money be spent? Create your monthly budget. You can prioritise by categorising expenditure into boxes, e.g.
  - Must-haves (food, rent/mortgage, car payments, phone bills, childcare, transport fare etc.)
  - Should-haves (clothes, entertainment etc.)
  - Could-haves
  - Want-to-haves

Dealing with disappointment

When I pray, I feel hope, but I expect God to answer immediately. Then, when he doesn't, I lose that hope again. This is the enemy's tactic though. God knows what you need and when you need it even better than you do. Whatever it is, do not lose hope. Just trust that he has your back and will always be on time.

Mary and Martha held out in the hope that Jesus would come to heal their sick brother. I can just imagine the kind of conversations they had with friends and neighbours in the days before Lazarus's death.

When Lazarus fell ill, I can imagine friends saying to Mary and Martha, "Send a message to Jesus to come and heal your brother. He loves you so much. You don't even know how lucky you are." Then, when Lazarus' illness took a turn for the worse, they might have said, "Didn't you send that message? Why didn't he come? Maybe he doesn't really have the power to heal. Or he just doesn't care."

Mary and Martha, fearful but still holding on to their slowly diminishing strand of hope, would have thought, "I hope he comes before Friday. I don't think Laz can hang on any longer. He could die soon." They know Jesus; he has never failed them. They trust him with all their hearts. Even at their lowest points they refuse to stop believing.

But when Lazarus dies, they retreat into themselves; hope dashed, faith lost, awash with pain, disappointment and a feeling of betrayal they can't seem to shake. "Oh, my heart is broken," I imagine Mary cried. "Jesus... How could he not be there when I needed him the most? It's over. Nothing can save Laz now."

But Jesus did show up and he revealed his power to them. He was saying to them, "Your ways are not my ways."

In the same way, I have come to realise that Jesus is never too late. He is always on time.

We're constantly setting deadlines for God. We say, "Oh God, please send me my husband before I turn thirty," or, "Please give us a child before the end of the year," or, "I need to get that job before the end of the month or else I'll lose my home/car." But Jesus smiles back at us, saying, "Just hold on, my child, just hold on."

Often, we try to resolve issues in our own power. Then, when it all falls apart, we run back to Jesus and he takes us back with arms wide open. Whatever you're dealing with, just take it to the Lord and wait on him with as much faith as you can muster. Whenever I start losing faith, I stop myself and think, "All I have to do is believe. What have I got to lose?"

What disappointment are you currently dealing with?

1. _____

How do you feel about it?

_____

What can you do to change the situation?

_____

Is there another disappointment you are currently dealing with?

2. _____

How do you feel about it?

_____

What can you do to change the situation?

_____

Fear in love

There is no fear in love. But perfect love drives out fear because fear has to do with punishment. The one who fears is not made perfect in love.

1 John 4:18 (NIV)

The one who knows you has the power to hurt you. Like in action movies, only someone who knows where the 'bullet wound' is knows where to apply enough pressure to inflict pain. So how do you open yourself up to love?

When you think of a wedding, you think, *love, beauty, life.* A survey was carried out in which the researcher asked the following question: "What is the first thing that pops into your head when you hear the word 'marriage'?" The responses he received are interesting. The only answers connected with love and happiness were from people who had never been married. The other responses varied from "hard work" and "responsibility" to "RUN!" and "divorce".

It's interesting that people work so hard to get into relationships, but once they're in one, it seems like they're trying to get out again! What is it that makes us look outwards when we're in a relationship? Is it the fact that our closest friend seems like she has a better deal? Or that the guy in the office, the one we've had a crush on for a while, suddenly seems to find us attractive now that we're in a relationship? Or is it that when we get to know our partner, we realise that he isn't the one for us?

But what if you've found the one, you've settled down into your 'happily ever after', yet something inside of you just seems intent on jeopardising the relationship and you feel you're unable to control it?

Here are some of the ways we push our partners away:

WITHOLDING AFFECTION

Do you find yourself reluctant to show affection to your spouse? Or do you stop doing the things they like? For a husband, it could be opening the door for his wife, or offering a foot or back rub whenever she's tired. For the wife, it could be preparing his meals.

When my husband and I were dating, I loved cooking for him. I would go to the market, buy fresh ingredients and spend hours in the kitchen. I did it because I wanted to. It continued in the early years of our marriage, but after a few years and two kids, full-time work and a bakery business, it started becoming unsustainable. Something had to give. Most nights I would come home too tired to care about food for myself, but I knew I had to feed the kids. I started saying, "My husband can sort himself out…" And I can assure you, he sorted himself out; the chicken shop on the high street knows him on a first name basis. Apparently, one day he mentioned his missus and they were shocked that he had a wife and yet showed up at the chicken shop almost every night. 'Sorting himself out' was so frequent that it became a habit. He had stopped being a priority to me.

BEING EMOTIONALLY UNAVAILABLE

Imagine that you used to be in a relationship where you got pushed away every time you reached out for affection. Now in your new relationship you're reluctant to reach out for fear of being pushed away, so instead you shut down and become unaffectionate.

It is important to open up to your spouse about your past experiences and your fears so that he can empathise. If he is more affectionate, he can be the one to initiate your affectionate moments.

NIT-PICKING

Do you find fault in everything your husband does? Do you feel that he never does anything right, no matter what his intentions are or how much effort he puts in?

In what ways do you push your partner away? Write them down here and make a conscious decision to avoid doing them.

1. _____

2. _____

3. _____

4. _____

When we open ourselves up to love our husbands in the right way, we're also opening ourselves up to receive love.

Mirroring

"Are you okay?" my husband would ask.

"Yes, I'm fine. Why do you ask?"

"You look upset about something," he would respond.

My expression indicated I was upset about something – but I couldn't identify what that might be. So instead I would say the first thing that came into my head so that my husband wouldn't think it was a natural expression for me to look angry. "I'm upset about..." We would hash it out – sometimes it went on for hours – analysing whatever had caused me to feel bad; all the while, at the back of my mind, I would be thinking, "This is all a waste of time. I'm not really upset."

One day I had an unexpected breakthrough.

As usual, my husband said, "You look upset. Did I do something wrong?"

This time, instead of answering, I looked intently at him and realised that he had the same expression on his face that he had just noticed on mine. So I said, "You know, I think I might just be mirroring your expression. Is something wrong?"

It turned out that something was indeed wrong and so we talked about it, but instead of my thing – where my problem was both made-up and ridiculous – this was a real issue.

I have become more aware of how we mirror each other over the years, and it can happen both ways. Sometimes when I see him looking angry, I check myself before asking if anything is wrong. I check that his expression and attitude isn't coming from the vibes I'm putting out and, if it is, then I adjust my attitude. If he has been mirroring me, I can see the same adjustment happening in him as well.

Being aware of this is also invaluable during an argument. The chances are that the moment you start raising your voice, your partner will raise his voice as well. This is especially useful for me as when my husband raises his voice just a little bit, it triggers something in me and I find myself shouting at the top of my voice. Sometimes, just taking deep, measured breaths and relaxing your facial expression and your body language can de-escalate an argument. It means that you have to be conscious and aware; as anger is the loss of control over your emotions, you have to reach deep and regain control.

More generally, mirroring refers to when someone subconsciously imitates another – whether that be their words, their gestures or their attitudes. Two good examples are yawning and smiling. Yawning is so contagious that just hearing a yawn can trigger the same reaction in you. Similarly, when someone approaches you with a smile, the natural reaction is to return the smile without even thinking about it.

Sometimes when I'm not in a good mood or perhaps just distant, worried about something or with a lot on my mind, my husband comes to me and doesn't say a word; he just smiles. I know what he's doing and sometimes I try to resist because I'm relishing the comfort of my mood too much to let go. But he persists and eventually I find myself mirroring his expression, not because I want to but because I feel compelled to. Sometimes that's all it takes to get me out of a bad mood.

> *If you have only one smile in you, give it to the people you love. Don't be surly at home, then go out in the street and start grinning 'Good morning' at total strangers.*
>
> *Maya Angelou*

Now I pay more attention to my body language with my husband, consciously putting out more positive vibes. Unfortunately, because of the issues we had early on in our marriage, I feel like the default setting for my face was anger and irritation and so now I have to make more of an effort to reset my face when I find it defaulting to its more negative setting.

The satnav phenomenon

> *I will strive to speak to other people the way I wish to be spoken to – with kindness, respect, and consideration.*[3]
>
> *Gregory L. Jantz*

My husband and I learnt to drive when we found out we were expecting our first child. After passing our driving tests, we bought a car and a satnav, a small Tomtom. However, because neither of us were used to driving or using the satnav, we found it confusing. For example,

---

[2] *https://www.goodreads.com/quotes/178794-if-you-have-only-one-smile-in-you-give-it*

[3] Gregory L. Jantz; *Hope and Healing from Emotional Abuse;* Revell (2013).

it would say, "In two miles, take the exit," but all we would hear is, "Take the exit!"

Can you imagine if your satnav was a real person giving you directions? I saw the movie 'Escape from Planet Earth' recently in which the navigation system, Ricky Gervais's voice, constantly gave unwanted advice and opinions. I was reminded of this another day on my way back home from work; I decided to try a different route, thinking it would take me home faster. The satnav 'lady' kept insisting that I should "stay in the right lane" but I ignored her and took the exit I had my mind set on, then held my breath as I waited for the inevitable re-planning of my route. I gasped as I realised that taking my exit had added twenty minutes to my journey and, not only that, there was so much traffic on the way that I suspected that the twenty minutes would be an underestimate. As I berated myself inwardly for such a foolish mistake, the lady's voice began to speak again, calmly, as if nothing had happened. "Stay in the right lane for the next three miles. This is your fastest route, and you will reach your destination by 18:20."

Yes, I know that no matter how many wrong turns I take, her tone will remain the same – but it made me wonder… What if my satnav could voice its opinion? I imagined the lady mocking me and telling the story about the idiot who was in such a hurry to get home and chose not to listen to the wise satnav and ended up spending an hour on a thirty-minute journey to her work colleagues during her lunch break.

And then I thought, what if it was the other way around? What if we took our cue from the satnavs? What if we had the same patience and gentleness in our voices?

My husband told me about a business venture he wanted to go into. His friend was doing it as well, and he sounded really excited about it. I tried to dissuade him by sending articles that highlighted why it was a bad idea, but he always found a way to counter every argument.

Eventually I caved in. "If it makes you happy, I'll back you all the way," I said to him.

In the end, it didn't work out and money was lost. I have to admit, it was difficult to hold back the "I told you so" as it bubbled under the surface of every meaningful look and loaded conversation. I fought it for days, and in the end, I found words that I hoped would convey my message without coming across as condescending.

"I need to tell you something," I said to him. I could already see his walls coming up, as you do when someone approaches you with those words. "I just want to let you know that with everything that happened, I don't hold it against you."

He paused as if trying to read the meaning behind my words. After a while he nodded. "I hear you and I really appreciate it."

We hugged and that was the end of it. Before I raised the subject, it was a heavy load on my mind; I was itching to say how I felt about the whole episode. The way I would have approached it in the past would have been to make him see that I had been right from the beginning and he should have listened to me. I'm not saying my approach was the best, but I needed to get a message across without making him feel bad about it. It was important for me to say it as much as I would like to believe that it was important for him to hear it. I felt like if I didn't say it, every time I was upset about something else, he might think it had something to do with what had happened. Or if I disagreed with a decision, the incident would hang over our heads, invisible but very present.

Gregory L. Jantz wrote that the ways to stop the I-told-you-so's slipping out is to internalise the statement, "I will strive to speak to other people the way I wish to be spoken to – with kindness, respect and consideration."[4]

---

[4] 'I told you so'; *Psychology Today.*
https://www.psychologytoday.com/experts/gregory-l-jantz-phd

CHAPTER NINE

Bring on the Drama

I DON'T KNOW WHAT CHANGED, I can't tell you exactly how it happened, but one day I found myself fighting back. I stood up for what I wanted and I made my voice heard, and it felt good. And afterwards my husband apologised to me. And I thought, "Really, I should do this more often." I now know that in a marriage, it is important that *both* parties have a voice. It was never my husband's intention for me to accept all his decisions, it was a choice that I made, but it was easier to resent him than to acknowledge my weakness. Instead of accepting that I was playing the victim and finding my voice, it was simpler to label him a bully and enjoy the self-indulgence I found in being a victim – yet it was all in my head.

Now we have our disagreements and I speak my mind, no matter how ridiculous it sounds. Leaving those thoughts rolling around in my head builds them up into a big deal, but speaking them out loud, more often than not, either exposes my grievances as not fact or helps me realise their insignificance.

Like me, so many people excuse their passive-aggressiveness as being considerate and compromising. However, compromising means meeting in the middle, as opposed to agreeing to everything without argument. A passive-aggressive person will keep quiet when a decision is being made but then, when it turns out it was a bad one, they'll be the first to say, "I knew that was going to happen..."

Let your voice be heard in your marriage. This doesn't mean you should raise your voice above your husband's but let him know where you stand on an issue. Saying nothing is a big cop-out. Any bad decision that affects your spouse will affect you too.

Be honest with your emotions

Speaking of baiting husbands, do you remember the story of Sarah, Abraham and Haggai?

Sarah and her husband have been trying for a child for a long time. One day, angels pay them a visit and they inform Abraham that he will bear a child. Sarah laughs but deep inside, she's hopeful.

Years pass and still no child, so Sarah starts thinking. "Wait a minute... God said *Abraham* will have a child. Maybe the child doesn't have to come from me. I just want my husband to be happy. Once he is happy, I will be happy as well. I can't bear the thought of him not having children just because there's something wrong with me.

On the other hand, the thought of him with another woman hurts so much I fear it will kill me. He's my husband and we love each other; that's all that matters."

A part of her counters, "*Is it?* He will go to the grave without an heir, his name will be synonymous with sterility across the land and it will be *your fault*."

She battles within herself.

So Sarah goes to Abraham. "My husband, my lord, love of my life, take my maid, Haggai; she will bear you a child. The child will be our child."

"Are you sure?" Abraham asks.

"Yes, yes, I'm sure. Your happiness is my happiness; your son will be my son also."

And so Abraham goes into a tent with Haggai.

I can imagine Sarah rolling from one end of her tent to the other in anguish, tears pouring down her face, as she grits her teeth and tears at her garment. "What have I done?" she laments.

Haggai comes in the next morning and the tension in the room could be cut with a knife. The two women avoid each other's gaze.

"Go away," Sarah finally says to her. "I don't need you this morning. Go and rest; you've had a rough night."

Haggai lowers her head and, without saying a word, leaves Sarah's tent.

Every night after that, Haggai goes into Abraham's tent. This goes on for over two weeks and Sarah dies a little more inside each time.

A few months pass and it is confirmed that Haggai is pregnant.

"My love, thank you for this gift. You have made me so happy. You're a noble and wise woman, and I will love you for ever," Abraham says to Sarah.

Sarah forces her lips to stretch into a smile. "Yes, I am happy too," she lies.

Perhaps Sarah's example may seem a little extreme, but as human beings, sometimes we refuse to acknowledge our emotions. Are you upset every time your husband speaks to 'that particular woman'? Be honest with how you feel about the things in your marriage. Not being honest will breed unhealthy resentment in your heart.

Sarah finally faces her emotions – but instead of taking responsibility, she cries out to Abraham, "You are responsible for the wrong I am suffering. I put my slave in your arms, and now that she knows she is pregnant, she despises me. May the LORD judge between you and me."

And Abraham responds, saying, "You know what? She's *your* slave. I'm not getting involved."

So Sarah mistreats Haggai and Haggai runs away with her little boy, Ishmael, to escape the harsh treatment. None of this would have happened if Sarah had been honest with her feelings in the first place.

The way you communicate your emotions is just as important as being honest about them. As much as you can, avoid the blame game. Don't say, "You are responsible for the wrong I am suffering." Distance yourself from any comments that make you out to be a victim and him a villain, as this brings up a defensive wall fast, and once the wall is up, it's hard to get your message through.

Focus on how you feel about the situation and paint a picture that will make it easy for your spouse to empathise with you. You're on the same team.

For better... or worse

Unless you have the best luck in the world, married life will come with its own sets of challenges.

We've had times when we didn't know what we would eat the next day and other times when we have had so much that we could afford to give away thousands of pounds. The worst thing you can do is expect everything to be rosy and then quit at the first sign of trouble.

Every marriage has its ups and down and I'm sure yours isn't any different!

FIGHT FOR YOUR MARRIAGE

By reading this book and other books on marriage, you're already taking steps towards fighting for your marriage. Too often in my generation, I have witnessed women with a *laissez-faire* attitude towards their marriage. Who will fight for your marriage if *you* won't do it? Imagine that your marriage is a precious gem; will you leave it out on the porch and hope that it will be fine? Or will you hide it in your innermost secret place, taking it out often to admire its beauty, polishing it to preserve its glimmer and shine?

DON'T STOP 'LEARNING YOUR SPOUSE'

You'll be amazed how much you still don't know about your spouse after several years of marriage. Find time to go out on dates, and if you can't afford to go out or can't find a babysitter, you can have your dates in the house after the kids have gone to bed. Turn your mobiles and TV off and just learn your spouse. If your husband was cloned and replaced, would you even notice? Do you know his most embarrassing experience or the best day of his life? Do you know where all his birthmarks are? Even if you feel that you know all there is to know, as human beings we're constantly changing and it would be wrong to assume that your spouse is the same person you got married to.

CHAPTER TEN

Dealing With Conflict

Focus on the solutions and not the problems

WHEN I'M DISSATISFIED WITH a situation at home, my first instinct is to react; to show anger or frustration. I start using phrases like, "You never..." or, "You always..." Over the years I noticed a pattern: whenever my spouse came to me with such statements, my defensive walls came up and not once did I ever admit that I 'never' or 'always' did something. Do you know why? Because at some point in the years we'd been married I had done those things at least once.

For example: "You never shut the fridge door properly." Come on! Surely, I must have closed that door at least nine out of ten times. You chose the one time I didn't and decided to make me into a fridge villain? That just will not fly!

And so, we get deeper into it, and it stops becoming about the fridge and progresses into, "You always treat me like I don't matter."

How did we diverge so far from the original topic?

It occurred to me that if I didn't like it when my husband spoke to me this way, why did I think it was okay to talk to him like that? I decided that things needed to change. So now I swallow my anger and frustration until such a time when something that *needs* to be done has not been done. Or, better still, *before* the time that that thing needs to be done, I say to my husband, "Please can you make sure that _____ [insert task here] gets done?"

Most times I get an "Okay." Sometimes, I get a "Why can't you do it?" Rarely do I get a "No." Job done! Mission accomplished! Headache and argument averted.

Focus on the end result

You and your spouse will react differently to different situations at different times, depending on many different circumstances such as who is performing the action, when they did what they did, what happened when they did it and associations you've had with that action in the past. You can control your reactions, however. We should not be slaves to our emotions and it's important to be conscious of the power we have over them, although I know it's easier said than done sometimes.

For example, if your spouse is upset about something and your immediate reaction is to match his tone, you can choose to do that or you can decide that no good will come out of both of you screaming at each other, take a step back, take deep breaths and count to ten in your head.

Sometimes it's still hard to respond without a heated argument developing. In such situations, I find it's better just to walk away. Pick up the conversation when you're both calmer and able to resolve the issue.

Before having the conversation, know what you want to achieve, in order to avoid drifting off into past mistakes and pointing fingers which lead to even more hurt and can create a rift in the relationship. For example, if you're upset that your husband spent the night in a club with his friends and you couldn't get through to him all night, the goal of the conversation might be to get him to accept that what he did was wrong and that he should consider your feelings next time. Or the goal could be to agree what time he should be home when he goes clubbing because it makes you worry when he stays out so late. Whatever you do, stick to meeting your goal. Your goal is not to abuse him or make him feel guilty. Never start with an accusation – if you do, it is likely that he'll erect strong defensive walls and then it will be harder for you to get your message across.

Not having a clear goal for a serious marital discussion is like a woman who decides to prepare a special meal for dinner. Without knowing what meal she wants to prepare, she heads to the market. She picks up some chicken, mushrooms, then she walks around the vegetable aisle and picks up a packet of sweet peppers. "I wonder if I need these?" she thinks as she places them in her basket. "Broccoli? Why not? Fish fillets? Hey, the more the merrier, right?" She gets to the till and realises that she doesn't have enough money to pay for everything she has. She scrapes through all her accounts, spills her coins and uses up the coupons in her bag to pay the bill. When she gets home, she decides that she wants to make chicken and mushroom pie – and why not? She has the chicken and the mushrooms, and a few extras that she doesn't need. Halfway through the meal preparation, she realises that she's missing a key ingredient: puff pastry.

Like this woman, you start picking up issues that have nothing to do with the end result you're trying to get to. The conversation goes off tangent so badly that it's hard to get back on track. And even if you succeed at steering the conversation back, defensive walls are up so high that no effective resolution is reached.

Recall a recent situation in which it would have been useful to have a game plan before a conversation.

_____

_____

_____

In hindsight, what would you have written in your plan?

_____

_____

_____

The in-law situation

Many movies depict mothers-in-law as difficult to get on with so it's easy to assume that every encounter with the in-laws will leave you tearing your hair out.

I remember when my husband told me he was going to introduce me to his mom. I knew they were close; they spoke on the phone often. In one week, they probably spoke more than I did to both my parents in a month, so I began to be concerned that I was dealing with a 'mummy's boy'. To make matters worse, I was almost two months pregnant. It wasn't my ideal scenario, but with shaky hands and shattered nerves, I agreed. I mean, what choice did I have? I braced myself for contempt and the inevitable "you want to trap my son into marriage" drama. But when I came face to face with my future mother-in-law, she wrapped her arms around me and showered me with love. I thought I was dreaming. The previous night had been spent tossing and turning, certain that this woman would hate me and that my boyfriend would have to break up with me because his mom said so, for nothing.

I have heard many more stories similar to mine. My mom and my sister-in-law (my brother's wife) get on so well that it would be easy to believe that she's her daughter. My sister has a great relationship with her mother-in law as well.

That said, while there are many great mother-in-law stories, I'm not so blind as to say that the not-so-great ones don't exist. Go into a relationship with your in-laws with an open mind. It helps if your spouse puts you first and will fight his family for you, but in my opinion, it is not *your* fight. Taking matters into your hands against his family has all the potential to backfire. The best you can do is maintain your integrity and an attitude of respect in the face of resistance from one or more of your in-laws.

Make your husband aware of the situation by sticking only to the facts. Do not escalate or exaggerate anything. Do not throw your emotions into the mix. Let your spouse choose the next steps to resolve the situation. Always remember that while they may forgive their son or brother, it might not be so easy for them to forgive you.

In our parents' generation, typically the man built the house and then brought his bride into the home and provided for his family. His parents and siblings felt they owned the house and that the bride was to remain subservient to them at all times, regardless of age. I witnessed my mom being disrespected by her in-laws when I was younger, and I didn't understand how she continued to bear it and maintain the respect and dignity she displayed.

Times have changed so much since then; women are bringing in equal provisions into the households and sometimes even more than the man brings in. In some homes, the woman has put down all or most of the deposit for the house. And so it flips a switch when an in-law comes to visit and expects the wife, who has to go to work and look after her family, to wait on them hand and foot. They treat the wife like a second-class citizen in her own home. More than once, I have heard women complain, "If only they knew who brings in the bacon in this home." My response is always, "That's not the way you want to win this fight."

To win, you have to be the bigger woman. Maintain an attitude of respect, but never accept the unacceptable. It is your home and your role should be acknowledged and respected, but I recommend leaving financial details out of the conversation.

What are the things that upset you about an in-law?

1. _____

2. _____

3. _____

4. _____

5. _____

Can you talk to your husband about them? Remember, be sensitive to his feelings and only stick to the facts. The goal should be for peace and not to create animosity.

Wearing the problems in your marriage like a badge of honour

You know when you're looking for sympathy or just an excuse to get out of anything, and you quote the problems in your marriage? Or your friends are talking about theirs and you feel like you can do one up on their marriage? I did this for a long time, and it only occurred to me recently how tasteless this is. Even situations that were not problems were trumped up to look like problems just to get attention.

Arguing in front of the kids

You know you shouldn't – you've read all the articles, you know how unhealthy it is for them – but somehow, when your triggers are being set off, all restraint flies out the window.

It is possible to form a habit of not arguing in front of the kids. If your children are old enough to be left alone, or if there's another adult in the house, you could go into another room or, preferably, out of the house altogether. My husband and I used to go into the car whenever we were about to argue.

Try as much as possible to communicate without raising your voice.

Recently I had my friend's kids over for a play date. One of them ran up to me, the others following closely behind.

"My mummy and daddy are always fighting."

"Yes," her sibling piped up, "they fight all the time."

"My mummy and daddy are always fighting too," my daughter said, not wanting to miss out on all the fun. They actually thought it was funny; they were laughing.

"Hey, when did you ever hear your dad and me argue?" I countered. I racked my brain for the last time we had argued at all, let alone in front of the kids.

"I don't know."

"It's not a nice thing to say, okay?" Then I turned to the other kids. "Just because Mummy and Daddy speak to each other in a loud voice, it does not mean they're having an argument, okay?"

"But…"

"Okay?" I insisted

"Yes, Aunty," they chorused.

They were barely out of the kitchen when I dug out my phone to call my friend. She was mortified. Now she goes on long walks with her husband or out to dinner to iron out their disagreements.

Arguing in front of your kids can have long-term adverse effects. Children need emotional security, and conflict in the home threatens that.

> *Children exposed to conflict between parents are at risk of a range of negative outcomes including: emotional and behavioural difficulties, trouble getting on with others such as peers or family members, problems settling and achieving at school, sleep difficulties, and poorer health.[5]*

That's something to think about when you feel like a kettle about to blow its whistle.

---

[5] Jenny Reynolds et al.; *Parental conflict: outcomes and interventions for children and Families;* @Policy Press; ISBN: 9781447315810

Working together to raise your children

We all have different childhood experiences. I come from a family with four children and we were each raised differently by our parents. My siblings and I are different people with varying behavioural characteristics. My parents found a way to communicate and relate with each of us according to our personalities.

You and your husband have had different childhood experiences and so it will stand to reason that you will not always agree on how to raise your kids. You deal with issues like:

- how to discipline the kids;
- the kinds of food they're allowed to eat;
- the movies they watch;
- the music they listen to;
- the decision to attend an independent or free school;
- the after-school lessons they should attend.

The list goes on.

I believe that whatever decision you make, your kids will turn out alright if the decision is made out of love and if love is present in the home.

Sometimes I may disagree with the way my husband handles a situation with the kids, but we have a rule to not criticise one another's parenting style in front of them. I give him a look or shake my head to show that I disagree, and then the issue is discussed properly when the kids are out of earshot.

Parents should strive to show a united front to the kids, to let them know that "pitting us against each other is futile". There have been times when I don't agree with a decision or a directive given to the kids by my husband. The worst thing for me to do would be to undermine his authority by giving a conflicting directive. In those situations, I discuss the matter with him out of their earshot whenever possible. If that's not possible, we communicate in our native language which the kids don't understand. If he agrees with me, he either rescinds his directive or permits me to do it on his behalf.

What areas of raising your children do you find difficult to come to an agreement with your spouse? (e.g. forms of discipline)

1. _____

Your reason: _____

His reason: _____

Possible compromise: _____

2. _____

Your reason: _____

His reason: _____

Possible compromise: _____

3. _____

Your reason: _____

His reason: _____

Possible compromise: _____

4. _____

Your reason: _____

His reason: _____

Possible compromise: _____

Don't take yourselves too seriously.

With looking after the kids, full time jobs and other life commitments, sometimes it's easy to forget to just take a step back and enjoy the moment. What if you're unable to pay that bill tomorrow? What if the kids don't get the grade you expected? Share laughs and build memories that will last a lifetime together. Your spouse may be here today, but you never know where they'll be tomorrow. Enjoy every moment you spend together and don't let temporary problems deprive you of your joy.

Early on in our marriage, my husband was very playful; he would grab me from behind while I worked in the kitchen or hide behind the door to scare me. And every time I would either swipe at him, telling him to leave me alone so I could concentrate on the task at hand, or scold him for trying to send me into cardiac arrest. Didn't he know that I had high blood pressure? His playfulness became less common and less intense until it reached the point where we just smiled politely to one another when our paths crossed between tasks.

I know now that I will never remember the chores that got done or the ones that didn't, but the happy memories we make together will last a lifetime.

List the ways in which you used to have fun with your spouse but haven't done in a while or as often as you would like.

1. _____

2. _____

3. _____

4. _____

5. _____

CHAPTER ELEVEN

Changing Your Spouse

HERE IS A VERY EFFECTIVE WAY of selling a product: create the illusion that having it will create pleasure or that not having it will create pain. This same approach can be used when trying to effect any kind of change.

I took a project management course after my master's degree. I'd heard it was easy to get a job as a project manager. So I studied for weeks and passed my practitioner exam. I was thrilled. Now on to the next part: getting a job. It took numerous interviews and eventually I landed an amazing contract with a major TV firm. After seven months, though, my contract ended. It was in the middle of the recession. One of my friends nagged me constantly about taking a Business Analysis course. I was resentful; I had just sat a professional exam and now this person was on my case to try something else. I loved working in project management, I had had a great time at my old job and I wanted something similar. We argued about it, but this friend was relentless. It was a bone of contention between us. My resistance to the change was so strong. My friend's insistence on the change only proved that my thoughts or what I wanted didn't matter.

The last time we argued about it, my friend made the following statement that helped change my mind: "It's not about just doing what you want. It's about keeping your options open. You've been trying for months now, and you haven't been called for an interview in that whole time. You have nothing to lose by trying something new. You can always go back if you don't like it. The last thing you want is to have to go back home (to Nigeria) because you can't get a job." The picture of me heading back to Nigeria in defeat was the incentive I needed to change.

As a parent, I'm even more familiar with using this tactic as a way to get my kids to do what I want them to do. I issue statements like, "If you don't get up right now, you're going to be late for school, and your teacher will not be happy with you," or, "If you do your revision, you'll get ice cream." The first statement promises pain; my daughter likes making her teacher happy and will do anything she can to make sure her teacher doesn't get upset with her. The second statement promises pleasure. In both cases, it has to be an appropriate form of pain or reward. If the child doesn't care about what her teacher thinks, I would have to employ a different image to elicit the required pain response; likewise, if the child hates ice cream, there is no motivation to carry out a task she doesn't want to perform.

My husband and I have had to change so much since we met. The thought of losing the other person due to stubbornness or pride was the pain picture we needed to change.

However, as much as we've changed for the better, we've also picked up bad habits along the way. So change isn't a one-time thing; it's constant. There will always be change as long as our conditions change, for example, we're getting older, having kids, having more kids, kids are getting older, etc.

As much as you work towards changing your spouse, your spouse has to *want* to change. To motivate them, the change needs to be to their advantage, not just for your benefit.

You too need to be open to change. Reason with empathy; how is your resistance to that change affecting your spouse? What do you have to lose by changing? How much effort will it require?

Is there something you would like to change about your spouse? Write down the consequences of not changing.

1. _____

2. _____

3. _____

4. _____

Now list the benefits that change will bring.

1. _____

2. _____

3. _____

4. _____

5. _____

Is there a habit you know you need to change?
Write down the consequences of not changing.

1. _____

2. _____

3. _____

4. _____

Now list the benefits that change will bring.

1. _____

2. _____

3. _____

4. _____

5. _____

Making Assumptions

We're prone to make assumptions based on past experiences. This isn't something you can change overnight. It could be your paranoia that your spouse is cheating because they always make calls in the car. Or that your spouse has something to hide because they always place their phones facing downwards.

Before your paranoia becomes fully blown, ask why they do what they do. You'll get a defensive response most of the time, so be careful how you ask. Explain where you're coming from, in order that your spouse is sensitive to your paranoia. Your spouse should be able to answer your question directly. If he doesn't, then you have to request a direct response. You can say, "Please help me understand. I trust you but I'm worried you're putting yourself in a compromising position."

I read a story online recently about a young lady who, suspecting that her boyfriend was cheating on her, plastered his car with sanitary pads. When she eventually confronted him about his infidelity, it turned out that he had been secretive because he was planning a surprise party for her... Before you assume the worst about your spouse, give him or her the benefit of the doubt and ask your most pressing questions directly.

What assumptions have you made in the past?

1. _____

2. _____

3. _____

4. _____

For each of the above, how did you deal with your assumption? For example, did you act rashly or did you confront your spouse?

1. _____

2. _____

3. _____

4. _____

Time of the month

I'd heard of PMS since I was a teenager. To me, it was a myth; an overused joke in US sitcoms where a lady is asked if she's on her period due to an erratic or irrational behaviour.

According to the NHS website, symptoms of PMS include acne, tender breasts, bloatedness, fatigue, irritability and mood changes. This varies according to the individual and, even then, the intensity of symptoms in one individual may vary over time. So, I knew about the acne, the bloating and tender breasts, but the combination of fatigue, irritability and mood swings in a new marriage can cause a lot of confusion especially if as a woman you're clueless as to the changes your body is going through.

A few days before my period, I would go through severe emotional dilemmas, at which times I couldn't stand my husband. (Everyone else was in the clear.) I found everything he did annoying, and during those times I would question how I had come to marry him. I could see him trying hard to make me happy, but it only served to worsen my guilt. I didn't understand what was going on.

During the times when I was dating, I may well have jeopardised a relationship based on how I felt during those times of the month. I criticised his appearance, the way he smiled and was generally dissatisfied with my immediate environment. I would go on cleaning sprees; everything felt dirty, nothing was right. And on top of that I had to deal with the soul-crushing fatigue. I never saw the pattern. I always wanted to communicate what I was going through but I didn't know how to without sounding cheesy or making him think I was looking for an excuse to be distant.

As soon as my period starts, it's like a weight being lifted, like clouds parting after heavy rains. All is well with the world, the sun starts shining again and I can hear the birds. The love that I feel for my husband rushes back in and I feel like a different person.

The embarrassing part is that my husband spotted the pattern before I did. One day he said, "Oh, you've started your period," with a huge grin on his face.

I looked at him, puzzled. He hadn't seen my period, so how could he know?

"Well, you've started smiling again."

That was when it clicked.

I had a conversation with my colleague about it the next day; I wanted to find out if it happened to everyone else or if it was just me. We compared notes on the craziest things we'd done during PMS and we realised that it was probably not the best time in a woman's cycle to make any significant emotional decisions.

Now that my husband and I understand what it is, it's made it easier for us to deal with it and I certainly feel less guilty when I'm on an emotional rollercoaster. At the same time, I try to be sensitive to his feelings as well.

Can you identify how PMS affects you and your relationship?

1. _____

2. _____

3. _____

4. _____

5. _____

CHAPTER TWELVE

Learning Forgiveness

Let go of past hurt and resentment

And be kind to one another, tenderhearted, forgiving one another, even as God in Christ forgave you.

Ephesians 4:32

SOMETIMES I START TALKING about something and find myself dipping into the past for an applicable reference, and as I'm standing in the past, all the hurts and mistakes my husband made start calling out my name, gleaming and glistening in the spotlight of my focus and attention. I can't help myself. I stick my hands elbow-deep in the muck and unearth those things that should remain buried. I know I should stop – it doesn't feel right – but romanticizing past hurts makes me feel like a victim and my spouse like the villain. I should stop, we've moved on and, to be fair, it is not as though I have been completely blameless. Looking into the history of our relationship, we've both done things to hurt each other, knowingly or unknowingly.

Bringing up past hurts is pointless and it doesn't do any good to open up old wounds. What can your spouse do about it now? If it's an apology you want, and you know that you would not be able to move on properly without it, then be open and request an apology – but be mindful of how you do it.

Holding on to resentment not only hurts the one you resent, it hurts you as well. In the first five years of marriage, resentment was a word that was bandied about in our home, and it mostly came from me. I was resentful over so many things but what it all boiled down to was that I hated myself for not standing up to the things I was unhappy

115

with. My husband would say something or make a decision that affected me but instead of tackling the issue, I would say, "Okay." The resentment festered until it became a living, breathing thing between my husband and me. I was addicted to the resentment; I say this because it got to a point where I was putting out bait to feed my resentment and most of the time he played into my hands. Sometimes I would be upset with him but would struggle to explain to myself what he had done to deserve my anger. It became the default setting in our relationship: the cold shoulder and the blank, vacant look.

We weren't in a marriage, it felt more like bondage, and some days I would fantasise about walking out the door, leaving everything I had and never looking back. Anything, even living on the streets, was better than living in bondage. But it was a self-induced bondage. All the time I kept silent when my husband made up rules and decisions. I did it because I wanted to avoid confrontation. To be fair to him, he always asked me what I thought.

"I want to hear your opinion," he would persist.

"No, it's fine. If that's what you want, we'll do it your way," I would say, blank expression on the outside but seething inside.

Holding on to resentment is tantamount to saying you're not human and therefore not susceptible to human error, because to live and breathe each day is to make mistakes. Forgive those who've wronged you and it will become much easier to forgive yourself when you make mistakes too. You are human, you will make mistakes, but it will not, should not, must not, define you. Pick yourself up, dust it off and start again.

We all make mistakes, and marriage reveals a lot of our flaws. Avoid holding your spouse's mistakes against them. It's hard to do, which is why it is important for us to make an effort at it. I try to let go of any misgivings I have regarding a decision my spouse makes. Ultimately the decision is up to both of us, and as long as the decision doesn't put any of us in danger, I try to understand his point of view before putting mine across, enabling us to come to a compromise. In the end, what is important to me is that we're together and happy. Where we are or what we have is a lot less important.

We ought not to look back, unless it is to derive useful lessons from past errors and for the purpose of profiting by dear bought experience.

George Washington

What things do you hold against your spouse that you find hard to let go of?

1. _____

2. _____

3. _____

4. _____

5. _____

Dealing with an infidelity

What would you do if you found out that your husband was cheating on you or had cheated in the past? I bet that's a question you hope you never have to answer – and so did my friend Chioma.

Chioma's husband admitted cheating on her a few months previously and she was brave enough to open up to a stranger who was writing a book about marriage. I felt her story was unique because she chose to forgive him and move on. She feels that because of his courage to come clean and her willingness to forgive and let it go, their marriage is even stronger than it was before.

"I don't even know where to start," she said, laughing uneasily. "I've never spoken to anyone about this."

"Let's just start from the beginning."

Chioma's marriage could have been described as uneventful. There was no drama, nor was there any excitement. She and her husband loved one another, their kids and God, and went to church regularly. She trusted him so much; he was a good man. She could have left him in a room filled with beautiful women and not felt any worry. He loved her and he loved and feared God; surely that was enough...

The mirage was swept away one beautiful autumn Saturday. The kids were away at a sleepover and Chioma had woken up with so much love and joy in her heart, she thought she would explode.

She felt like having a cup of coffee so she asked him if he wanted one and he said no. It was the first time he'd ever said no to a cup of coffee but she didn't think anything of it. He eyed her coffee as she walked past him with a steaming cup and a plate of biscuits.

"Hey, you said you didn't want one," she said, thinking he was regretting his decision not to take her up on her offer. Little did she know that he was more worried about the coffee ending up *on* him.

"No, I'll get it myself."

She shrugged and set down her coffee and biscuits on her bedside table. Getting into bed and snuggling into the duvet, she grabbed the remote and turned the TV on. 'My Wife and Kids'! Could the day get any better? This was the first time in as long as she could remember that she was getting a lie-in. No kids, coffee and biscuits, 'My Wife and Kids' on TV. She was in mummy heaven.

Her husband sat down on the bed. She felt his eyes on her, so she glanced at him and then back at the TV. She wondered why he still didn't have his coffee mug. Then she looked at him again and noticed he had tears in his eyes.

"What is it?" she asked, worry and concern bubbling up to the surface. She set her mug down and turned the TV off, turning to give him her full attention.

"I haven't been completely honest with you," he started, and then he burst into uncontrollable sobs.

She gathered him into her arms and held him tight. Alarm was fast replacing concern. So many things ran through her mind. She wondered if it was about money; had he got them into debt and now they were in trouble? Or had he started a business she didn't know about and now he was in trouble? Not once did she consider that it was another woman.

He disentangled himself from her embrace and slid to the floor on his knees. "I'm so sorry, please forgive me," he said.

"It's okay, I forgive you," she answered, not really sure what she was supposed to forgive. But whatever it was, she felt surely ready to forgive him. He looked as though he was in pain and, at that moment, all she wanted was to take that pain away.

He proceeded to tell her about all his indiscretions. It had started ten months ago and, at that time, he had been with three women. They had been one night stands, women he had met at parties. It was his fault; it was their fault.

"You mean... you actually had sex?" she asked him, struggling to believe her ears.

"Er... yes." He appeared confused at her naïve question.

In her wildest dreams, she'd never imagined that he would be the one that would cheat. It felt weird; it felt like it was happening to someone else and not to her. She just couldn't imagine her husband with someone else; holding her in his arms, kissing her, all the things he did with Chioma, his wife.

She tried to be honest about her emotions, she searched for the anger, and the pain, the hurt, any of the negative emotions she expected to feel, but they were absent. All she felt was an immense love for this man that knelt shattered before her.

"There must be something wrong with me," she thought.

She asked him all the questions that burned in her head. What were their names? How did he meet them? When did it start? When was the last time? Who made the first move? Did he use contraceptives? Were they married women? Did they still keep in touch? Were there any feelings involved?

"If you need some time alone, I'm happy to do anything. I can go and find somewhere to stay for a week or more if you want," he offered.

"No," she replied. "I don't need you to go anywhere. I forgive you." Then she added, "Yeah right, even if anyone *was* going anywhere, it would be me. You're not leaving me with the kids and getting a free holiday."

And she was true to her word; she forgave him immediately. It felt as though she had got her husband back, even though she hadn't known he'd been lost. They'd been 'happily married' in every sense, but somewhere along the line, they'd begun to take each other for granted and it had become the norm. That morning, Chioma felt like a veil had been lifted off her eyes and the first time in a long time, she truly *saw* her husband, flaws and all, and she loved him even more.

She held him in her arms and he was shocked that she wanted even to be in the same room as him, let alone touch him.

"I can't believe we're here. I already saw myself with bags packed, trying to find a place to stay."

"I could never throw you out," Chioma said, and she meant it, "but why did you tell me?" It didn't make any sense to her. Why didn't he just keep covering it up? She had never suspected he was cheating on her and probably never would have found out.

"I felt God battling with me," he explained. "I was afraid that something bad would happen if I didn't come clean. I was willing to risk not having you and the kids in my life, rather than have something bad happen to me or you because of something I did. It was by far the hardest thing that I've ever had to do. I know now that I was a fool; I love you even more and I'm so grateful to God for the kind of woman you are. How is this possible? How can you forgive me so easily?"

"It's easy," she replied. "I love you. I know that I married a flawed human being, prone to making mistakes, but I believe that you're sorry and repentant."

Later that day, when she was alone, she started to have worrying thoughts. Was she was letting him off the hook too easily? Was she really sure it was what she wanted? What if he decided to continue his indiscretions because he felt she would just forgive him again? What if she was just in shock and would feel different later?

She picked up her phone and googled, "My husband cheated on me, what should I do?"

Her search came up with lots of forums, women not knowing what to do after they had found their husbands out. She scanned through various posts, trying to find one that could relate to what she was feeling. Every post she read had a common thread: they had caught their husbands in the act; some were remorseful and some denied it outright. She found none that said their husband had just confessed because he couldn't live with the guilt anymore.

In one of the posts, a woman chose to forgive her husband and work on their marriage. She wrote about all the hurt and the pain and not being able to trust her husband anymore. The replies to her post agreed with her, saying it would take time for the wounds to heal. The responses were from women and men who had been cheated on by their spouses.

Chioma searched herself once again for all these emotions but she couldn't feel any wounds, pain or hurting; just love and joy. She began to feel that there must be something wrong with her. "You're a fool," a voice inside said. "He's playing you. How do you know he's telling you everything?"

She tried picturing what it would feel like to be single again, to be free to do whatever she wanted without having to discuss it first with her husband, and it felt good, In fact, it felt exhilarating and for one moment, she was tempted to let him go. But she loved him, and she recognised the foolishness of letting her husband go for doing something that she wasn't even upset about.

That evening, her husband came home with flowers and a 'thank you' card. She read the beautiful words he'd written in the card and set it down.

"Thank you so much," he said, gathering her up in his arms.

"Don't thank me yet," she responded, pulling out of his embrace. She watched fear creep into his eyes. "I need the phone numbers of all the women."

"But..."

"Please, I need to talk to them. I need to be sure you're telling me the truth."

"Okay, I'll do whatever you want. What if they're rude or they don't want to talk to you?"

"That's fine. Then I'll leave them alone." She watched him closely, wanting to see if he would try to protect any of the women, but he didn't.

"Is there anything you want to tell me before I call any of these women?" she then asked, looking him in the eye.

"No. I've already told you everything," he insisted.

She sent a message to the first woman, telling her that she wanted to speak with her about her relationship with her husband. At first the woman was on the defensive and so Chioma tried to put her mind at ease by telling her that she had forgiven her; all she wanted were some answers. The woman opened up to her about the affair and the next day the woman sent Chioma a message thanking her. She vowed to never contact her or her husband again.

Chioma made a decision to let it go and put it all in the past; to move on and forget that it happened. But it was hard to forget; sometimes all she could see when she looked at him were images of him with other women. She couldn't understand how he could bring himself to do what he did. At the time, Chioma wished she could confide in someone, but she felt the need to protect him. If she couldn't keep her own secret, what hope did anyone else have of keeping it to themselves?

As the days passed, her heart ached and she began to realise that she had been in denial. She began to feel the hurt and the pain, like it was a gaping wound in her chest. Every time she felt this pain, Chioma would pray to God to protect her heart, to help her remember the love and the joy she had once felt. The pain would go away but it always came back. More than ever, she was determined to stick to her guns as she fought for her family to remain together. Chioma and her husband decided to seek counselling from a professional, someone who didn't know who they were but would do whatever necessary to see their marriage healed. They found Holy Trinity Brompton's 'Marriage' course[6], which went a long way in helping them rebuild their relationship.

"How was it so easy for you to forgive him?" I asked Chioma

"In my limited understanding, I think it was God. The timing was so apt; the love I felt for him that morning was so unusual that I could have forgiven him anything. Also, I knew that it wasn't about me. It wasn't about me being a terrible wife, or letting myself go physically or not paying enough attention to him. It was about him being weak and falling into temptation. I was secure in who I was and in our relationship."

"So the kids had nothing to do with your decision?"

"There were so many factors involved in my decision. It was the life I was living then (and now), which I absolutely loved, versus a foreign life with my kids crying for their dad and having to juggle holidays and parental responsibility. Two households, two sets of bills, splitting childcare and all that. Having to deal with a new stepmom to my kids and all other headaches that come with divorce. But all that aside, ultimately, I made my decision based on how I felt, not out of fear."

"Why did you choose not to tell anyone?"

"It was a hard decision to make because there were so many things I wanted to say that I didn't want to say to his face. I also wanted reassurance that I was doing the right thing. A sad part of me wanted to know that I wasn't alone – that someone else I knew had gone through it and decided to still give their marriage a shot and that it had worked out in the end. Most of all, I didn't want anyone to try to change my mind or my decision. I also wanted to protect him from being judged

---

[6] See *www.themarriagecourses.org*

and disrespected. Only when I was sure of my decision did I open up about it to someone I trusted."

"Did you think of getting your own back?"

"I did," Chioma laughed. "The day before it happened, I had listened to the 'I Bust the Windows Out Your Car' song by Jazmin Sullivan. I thought, what if I rammed his car into a wall, or what if I just drove head-on into oncoming traffic? But those were fleeting thoughts and not once did I think that I would actually do it. I also thought about a guy that I knew liked me – what if I went to his house and just did the same thing my husband had done to me? Again, I knew it would be foolish and I would be hurting myself more than I would be hurting my husband if I went down that route. Two wrongs don't cancel each other out; they just make for two miserable people."

"I bet it affected the trust in your relationship."

"It's funny that you mention it but no, I still trust him. I know it sounds naïve, but whether I choose to trust him or not, I have no control over what he does in my absence. So I have a choice. Do I want to stay in this marriage and live like a crazy woman? Constantly calling his phone to find out where he is or what's he's doing? Looking through his phone and going through his things to try and catch him out again? Or do I want to live in peace and believe that he loves me and take his word for it that he'll never repeat his mistakes? I chose trust. By being insecure, I run the risk of pushing him away, but by choosing to trust, I'm letting him know that his mistakes don't define him. He is still the man I used to know. I'm impressed by his courage to come clean even though he didn't have to. I don't know if I would have had the same courage if the tables were turned. So I guess the short answer is no, this has not affected the trust. I dare say it has heightened it because now we are more open, knowing the dangers of keeping secrets from each other. After I told him I forgave him, he said he wasn't afraid to tell me anything now because of the maturity with which I handled his indiscretions."

Not all cases of infidelity end with a happily ever after. I met Danielle at a book writing conference. We were all asked to introduce ourselves and our book. I stood up and said, "Before I introduce my book, I would just like to admit that I am no expert on marriage. I have only been married six years."

A beautiful lady sitting in front of me turned around to face me and said, "I was married for six years when my marriage broke up."

I was interested in hearing her story and she was happy to share it with me. At the end of the workshop, I sat with her over a cup of coffee.

Danielle had found out her husband was cheating on her with a family friend when she went through his phone messages. Her initial reaction was to throw him out of the house. Hours later, after she had thought it over, she made up her mind that she would forgive him and try to make it work. She contacted her then husband to give him the news and his response stunned her. He was choosing to stick with the other woman. The woman's husband had found out about the affair and had left her, so she was "fragile and vulnerable" and "needed him".

"But what about me?" Danielle cried, her heart breaking into irreparable pieces as she watched the life she had built for seven years crumble before her eyes. "What about the children?"

Her kids were still babies; how could he just turn his back on them?

Final words

If your spouse is truly remorseful and loves you and wants to work on your marriage, you owe it to yourself and to your kids to give it another chance. Chioma has never regretted the decision she made to stay in her marriage and work on it. In fact, she and her husband are more in love now than they have ever been. He is more attentive and romantic, tells her that he loves her all the time and they make an effort to show how much they mean to each other every chance they get.

But be careful; don't just let things slide. Work on some ground rules together to make sure that the situation never repeats itself. Seek marriage counselling, from church or any other reputable marriage counsellor. Work through this thing together, write down the things both of you want or desire from your marriage. Set time out regularly – weekly or monthly – to review if both of you are fulfilling each other's needs.

Most importantly, start out on a clean slate; if you choose to forgive, you have to forgive completely. Abstain from bringing up your spouse's weakness and throwing it in their face. It might be tempting to do during an argument or when you're trying to get your own way. Forgive, and make the effort to forget that the indiscretion ever happened.

Be careful what you say about the situation and to whom you say it. If you chose to forgive your spouse, you might want to refrain from mentioning it to your close friends and family. It may be easier for you to forgive and to let it go – you know and love your spouse – but it may be a lot harder for your family or friends to forgive him. The last thing you want is to be caught in the middle when all you want to do is move on. Speak to someone you trust to counsel you objectively, and pray for God's strength and guidance.

Not every instance of an affair will be the same. I am careful not to judge a woman's actions after her heart and home have been broken, her hopes and dreams destroyed and her trust betrayed. Chioma and her husband were able to move past his indiscretions and try to make their marriage work, but for Danielle, she wasn't even given the option. If you ever find yourself in a similar situation, just remember that you are not alone. So many men and women have stood where you are and they have come through. Time will heal your wounds and in time you will overcome. Seek help from the people close to you, people you trust. Do not shut them out and don't close up your heart.

If you're going through a similar situation, the most important thing you can do is to remember that it is not your fault. It is not your lack of attention that pushed your husband into another woman's arms; he could have asked you for it. It's not the rolls of skin around your mid-section or the fact that you're a terrible cook. The blame for an infidelity lies only with the unfaithful party. Dealing with a broken heart is hard, and the best way to protect your heart is to submit it to God.

Sometimes it hurts even more when we pore over a bad situation with regret and should-have-dones. Knowing that everything that happened is outside your control, acknowledging that you're powerless to go back in time to fix anything, relinquishing control and submitting the future to the one who is able to see all, know all and do all things, will go a long way on the journey to your healing. He sees you and he has your best interests at heart.

When we got married, my husband and I used to pray that God would be the third strand in the knot binding us together. I didn't really understand what it meant then but it's getting clearer every day. For example, let's say I meet someone that I feel an attraction to and over time I come to realise that he feels the same way. I love my husband, but here is a person with whom I share a strong mutual attraction. To make matters worse, I feel that he really understands me. This is the 80/20 principle I mentioned in Chapter 4 – that 20%, he has it in spades! And surely, I understand basic mathematics, 80 is greater than 20, but oh, I've missed that 20%. I've missed it bad. A man that likes to do all the things I like to do but my husband has no interest in! After a while, all I can see is the 20% in my mind. I have inflated it into 1000%! The glasses are rose-tinted. I can literally smell the roses on the other side. The draw is potent, I can't resist it, and when I get to that crossroad, that point of no return, I hesitate. Should I turn back now or go ahead? I really want to go ahead, so I try to convince myself. I know I love my husband; I don't want to see him hurt; going ahead will tear my family apart. I will not just be letting myself down but also my family and friends... but what if I'm discreet? No one ever need know. No one will ever find out.

> *For there is nothing hidden that will not be disclosed, and nothing concealed that will not be known or brought out into the open.*
>
> *Luke 8:17 (NIV)*

With God as the third strand, you will not just be cheating on your husband, you'll also be cheating on a jealous God, a consuming fire, and he knows what you're about to do even before you do it.

If you're the one who's been unfaithful, my only advice would be to find the best way to confess to your spouse. There is nothing hidden under the sun and, like Chioma's story, it was easier for her to forgive because he came clean. Imagine how different the story would have been if Chioma had found out about the affairs on her own. Come clean completely; this is not the time to hide anything or to play any mind games. At this point, the trust is fragile and if your marriage is going to get a second chance, you need to start from a clean slate. Pray, pray and pray again before you have that conversation with your spouse. Whatever you do, don't make any excuses or try to blame it on your spouse or on the other party. Own up to your mistake, and when you ask for forgiveness, be sincere. No one can predict how your spouse will react; you need to decide if you require a third party present when you come clean.

If your spouse decides to forgive you and move on, usually the worst casualty is the trust. Be prepared to be open about everything you do and everywhere you go, until your spouse is able to trust you again. Remember that your spouse is hurting, so be sensitive towards his/her feelings.

You can find out what other people have done in your situation and how it worked out. In 'Forsaking all Others'[7], Esther Anderson boldly confesses her indiscretion and in 'Unfaithful: Hope and Healing After Infidelity'[8] Gary and Mona Shriver share their story of working it out to get to a place of healing.

---

[7] Esther Anderson; *Forsaking All Others;* Onwards and Upwards (2016); ISBN 978-1-910197-91-2

[8] Gary and Mona Shriver; *Unfaithful: Hope and Healing After Infidelity;* David C Cook Publishing Company (2009); ISBN 978-1434765338

Conclusion

MARRIAGE CAN BE A BED OF ROSES but, as this book has demonstrated, *you have to be willing to accept the thorns.* Because we're all human and no one is perfect, there will be sharp moments.

The enjoyment you get out of marriage will ultimately depend on how much work you're willing to put in to prune those thorns...

Related Books by the Publisher

Forsaking All Others
Esther Anderson

ISBN 978-1-910197-90-5

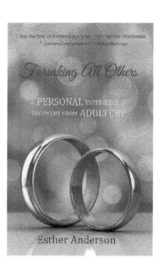

With openness and realism, Esther Anderson tells of her fall into adultery and the painful process of confession, recovery and healing. With God there is "hope in recovery" and "failure is not final".

With much practical advice and wisdom learnt from experience, this book is a vital guide for marriage counsellors and all those affected by an adulterous relationship.

Bachelorette to Bride
Natasha Peto

ISBN 978-1-911086-51-2

Marriage is one of God's greatest gifts to us. It is one of the most blessed and exciting events in a woman's life, but there is also a sense of entering the unknown. Becoming a wife can feel simultaneously like a great privilege and a tall order! This book has been written by a young bride, in the hope that she might provide some insight into the world of marriage for those who are thinking about marrying young. Natasha Peto unpacks the experiences, joys and challenges faced by the new bride, and offers helpful, practical advice that will help a young couple to enjoy their early married years together to the full, and to grow in intimacy and understanding towards one another.

Books available from all good bookshops and from the publisher:
www.onwardandupwards.org